Conquer Grammar

GRADE 2

Table of Contents

Introduction 5

Nouns
Singular and Plural Nouns 8
Irregular Plural Nouns 9
Proper Nouns 11
Collective Nouns 14
Possessive Nouns 15

Verbs
Present Tense Verbs 18
Past Tense Verbs 20
Irregular Past Tense Verbs 21
Future Tense Verbs 25
Verb Tenses 27

Subject-Verb Agreement
Collective Nouns with Matching Verbs 29
Singular and Plural Nouns with Matching Verbs 30

Pronouns
Personal Pronouns 31
Possessive Pronouns 33
Indefinite Pronouns 35
Reflexive Pronouns 37

Adjectives and Adverbs
Adjectives 39
Adverbs 43
Adjectives and Adverbs 45
Comparatives and Superlatives 47

Prepositions and Conjunctions
Prepositions 50
Conjunctions 51

Articles and Demonstratives
Articles 52
Demonstratives 53

Punctuation
Commas in Series 54
Commas in Dates and Series 55
Commas in Introductory Phrases and Clauses 56
Commas in Greetings 57
Commas in Closings 58
Commas in Greetings and Closings 59
End Marks 61

Contractions
Contractions 63
Contractions and Possessive Nouns 68

Capitalization
Capitalize Titles and Names, Days, and Months 70
Capitalize Geographic Names 71
Capitalize Holidays 73
Capitalize Geographic Names and Holidays 74

Sentences
Sentence Types 75
Simple Sentences 77
Compound Sentences 80
Combine Sentences 87

Language
Dictionaries 88
Formal and Informal Language 91

Answer Key 92

Introduction

This book is designed to help students have a better understanding of grammar, the fundamental organizing principle of language. The standards for most states as well as the Common Core State Standards require that students "Demonstrate command of the conventions of standard English grammar usage when writing and speaking." Students who understand how to use proper grammar are better able to say what they mean when writing and speaking.

Each of the 64 worksheets in this book reinforces a grade-appropriate grammar topic. The book is organized by parts of speech and other key topics. The goal is to equip students with an understanding of grammar so they can communicate more effectively.

How to Use This Book

Here are just a few of the many ways you can use this book.

Grammar Mini-Lessons: The most basic way to use this book is as a source of grammar mini-lessons. Write the grammar rule on the board. You can copy this straight from the gray box found on each worksheet. Introduce the rule, explain it, and then give examples. See if students can come up with their own examples. Then have students complete the worksheet. You can ask students to complete the worksheets individually or with partners, depending on ability levels. Check for understanding.

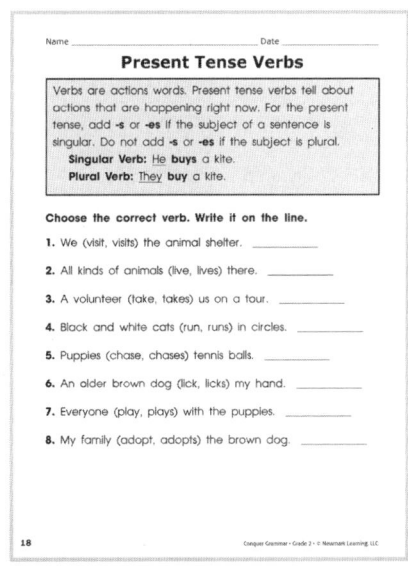

Grammar Reinforcement: After you have taught students a particular grammar rule, you can use these worksheets to give students the practice they need to reinforce their knowledge of the skill.

Grammar Assessment: The worksheets can serve as a formative assessment tool to show you where students might need additional teaching. Worksheets can also serve as a final assessment to confirm that students have mastered a particular rule.

Beyond the Book

There are myriad ways in which you can extend the lessons in this book. The goal is to keep the learning fun and interactive. Here are several ideas to get you started.

- Find examples of the grammar rules you are studying in books you read in class. Point out these examples to students. Then send students on a grammar-rule scavenger hunt to find examples themselves. You can expand the search area to books students read at home and in magazines, newspapers, notices around school, advertisements—anywhere there are written words. The more places students see the rule being used, the better.

- Ask students to practice using specific grammar rules in their own writing. For example, if you are studying a particular type of punctuation, have students use that punctuation in their writing. They can even go back and revise old work using knowledge gained from learning new grammar rules.

- Create a short daily exercise in which students are asked to use a recently learned grammar rule to correct a sentence that is written on the board. Students love correcting others' mistakes!

Key Tips for Teaching English Learners

The rules of grammar vary between languages. This can make learning English grammar particularly difficult for English Learners. It is helpful to know where the grammar rules between languages differ enough to cause a fair amount of confusion. Here are some of those areas.

Word Order	In languages such as Spanish, Farsi, Arabic, and Korean, word order in sentences may differ from that of English.
Verbs	In English, verbs are inflected for person and number. (*Everyone cooks food. She has a large cat.*) Verbs are not inflected for person and number in Vietnamese, Hmong, Korean, Cantonese, and Mandarin. (*Everyone cook food. She have large cat.*)
Nouns	Nouns and adjectives use different forms in English. (*They felt safe in their home. They were concerned about safety.*) In Spanish, Hmong, Cantonese, and Mandarin, speakers use the same form for nouns and adjectives. (*They felt safety in their home.*)
Possessive Nouns	In English, we add an apostrophe and *s* to most singular nouns, or an apostrophe only to proper, plural names that end in *s*, to show possession. In Spanish, Vietnamese, Hmong, and Tagalog, possession is shown using *of*. It is always *of Holly*, not *Holly's*.
Plural Nouns	Nouns become plural after a number greater than one in English. (*We go home in two weeks. They are bringing five shirts.*) In Vietnamese, Hmong, Tagalog, Korean, Cantonese, Mandarin, and Farsi, there is no change in the noun following a number. (*We go home in two week. They are bringing five shirt.*)
Adjectives	Adjectives precede the nouns they modify in English (*the blue flower*). In Spanish, Vietnamese, Hmong, Farsi, and Arabic, adjectives follow the nouns they modify (*the flower blue*).
Pronouns	In English, there is a distinction between subject and object pronouns. (*He gave it to me. We spent time with her.*) In Spanish, Vietnamese, Hmong, Cantonese, Mandarin, and Farsi, there is no distinction. (*He gave it to I. We spent time with she.*)
Prepositions	The use of prepositions in other languages differs from those used in English. (English: *The movie is on the DVD.* Spanish: *The movie is in the DVD.*)
Articles	Indefinite articles are used consistently in English. (*She is a brilliant scientist. He is an electrician.*) In Spanish, Hmong, Tagalog, Cantonese, and Mandarin, indefinite articles can be omitted. (*She is brilliant scientist. He is electrician.*)

Name _____ Date _____

Singular and Plural Nouns

> Singular nouns tell about one person, place, or thing.
> Plural nouns tell about more than one person, place, or thing.
> Add **s** to the end of most nouns to make them plural.
> For nouns ending in **x**, **z**, **s**, **sh**, or **ch**, add **es**. For nouns ending in a consonant and **y**, change the **y** to **i** and add **es**.
>
>   one bat   two **bats**
>   one box   three **boxes**
>   one guppy   two **guppies**

Choose the correct noun. Write it on the line.

1. I want two (pony, ponies). _____

2. Mom has one (car, cars). _____

3. We bought three (dress, dresses). _____

4. We have two (bird, birds) as pets. _____

5. I use my (brush, brushes) to paint. _____

6. The (fox, foxes) is orange and white. _____

7. I want a (puppy, puppies). _____

8. Look at the family of (bunny, bunnies). _____

Name _____ Date _____

Irregular Plural Nouns

> A plural noun names more than one person, place, or thing. Regular plural nouns end in **s**. Irregular plural nouns do not have any spelling rules or patterns. Some examples of nouns and their irregular plural forms include: **person/people, mouse/mice, child/children, cactus/cacti, goose/geese, shelf/shelves**.

Choose a noun from the box to complete each sentence. Write it on the line.

geese	shelf	children	cactus
cacti	child	goose	shelves

1. There are thirty happy _____ on the playground.

2. The _____ are filled with art supplies.

3. We read a book about a flock of _____.

4. We have two _____ growing in the classroom.

Rewrite each sentence with an irregular plural noun.

5. The four white mouse run across the floor.

_____

6. Many person ate the cake at my party.

_____

Conquer Grammar • Grade 2 • © Newmark Learning, LLC   9

Name _____ Date _____

Irregular Plural Nouns

A plural noun names more than one person, place, or thing. Regular plural nouns end in **s**. Irregular plural nouns do not have any spelling rules or patterns. Some examples of nouns and their irregular plural forms include: **foot/feet, calf/calves, wolf/wolves, tooth/teeth, life/lives, woman/women**.

Choose a noun from the box to complete each sentence. Write it on the line.

| life | teeth | wolf | calf |
| tooth | calves | lives | wolves |

1. The _____ were born in spring.

2. Dogs bark, but _____ howl.

3. The _____ of a tiger are sharp.

4. Cats do not really have nine _____.

Rewrite each sentence with an irregular plural noun.

5. Seven woman work on the farm.

   _____

6. There are two goose in the lake.

   _____

Name _____ Date _____

Proper Nouns

Proper nouns name specific people, places, or things. Each main word of a proper noun should begin with a capital letter.

People	Places	Things
Roger	Australia	Pacific Ocean
Taylor	Wyoming	United States
Fred	Delaware	National Zoo

Underline the proper noun in each sentence.

1. I moved from Columbus.

2. My best friend is Rose.

3. He took a trip to Mount Rushmore.

Choose a proper noun from the box to complete each sentence. Write it on the line.

Washington, D.C.   Lincoln Memorial   Amelia

4. I visited my friend _____.

5. She lives in _____

6. We went to the _____.

Conquer Grammar • Grade 2 • © Newmark Learning, LLC

Name _____   Date _____

Proper Nouns

Proper nouns name specific people, places, or things. Each main word of a proper noun should begin with a capital letter.

People	**Places**	**Things**
Rahul	California	Statue of Liberty
Thomas	New York	Central Park
Mia	Washington, D.C.	White House

Underline the proper noun in each sentence. Then write the proper noun correctly on the line.

1. I visited the city of austin. _____

2. We made pie with aunt kate. _____

3. We live on brodie lane. _____

4. He walks along walnut road. _____

Read each sentence. Then rewrite it correctly on the line.

5. The american museum of natural history is amazing!

   _____

6. I can't wait to visit utah again!

   _____

Name _____ Date _____

Proper Nouns

> Proper nouns name specific people, places, and things. Each main word of a proper noun should begin with a capital letter.
>
> | **People** | **Places** | **Things** |
> |---|---|---|
> | Emily | Kansas City | Brooklyn Bridge |
> | Ed Hall | New Mexico | Memorial Day |
> | Mrs. Chopra | Canada | Washington Monument |

Underline the proper noun in each sentence. Then write the proper noun correctly on the line.

1. My family went on a trip to nevada. _____

2. We saw hoover dam the next day. _____

3. We hiked down the grand canyon. _____

4. Our guide was named dan smith. _____

Read each sentence. Then rewrite it correctly on the line.

5. The festival is on main street.

   _____

6. We will visit mrs. adams next week.

   _____

Conquer Grammar • Grade 2 • © Newmark Learning, LLC

Name _____   Date _____

Collective Nouns

A collective noun names a group of people, places, or things. A collective noun is singular even though it names more than one.

A group of . . .	is called a . . .
students	class
mountains	range
birds	flock

Underline the collective noun in each sentence.

1. I see a bunch of flowers.

2. Is that a bundle of hay?

3. The flock of birds fly together.

Replace each noun in the parentheses ( ) with a collective noun from the box. Write it on the line.

crew	choir	class

4. The (sailor) cleaned the ship. _____

5. The (singer) sang a song. _____

6. The (student) passed the exam. _____

Name _____ Date _____

Possessive Nouns

A possessive shows ownership. Add an apostrophe and **s** to the end of a singular noun to form a possessive. For a plural noun that ends in **s**, add an apostrophe after the **s** to form a possessive.

Singular Possessive	**Plural Possessive**
Mom's ring	**girls'** shirts
store's parking lot	**customers'** carts
pond's water	**lakes'** shores

Circle the correct possessive. Write it on the line.

1. The _____ front door is red.   school's   schools'

2. The _____ faces are friendly.   teacher's   teachers'

3. Our _____ pet is a guinea pig.   classroom's   classrooms'

4. The _____ desks are new.   student's   students'

Rewrite each sentence. Replace the underlined words with a possessive.

5. I like <u>the cat that belongs to Lila</u>.

_____

6. <u>The shoes of the boys</u> are clean.

_____

Name _____   Date _____

Possessive Nouns

> A possessive shows ownership. Add an apostrophe and **s** to the end of a singular noun to form a possessive. For a plural noun that ends in **s**, add an apostrophe after the **s** to form a possessive.
>
> | **Singular Possessive** | **Plural Possessive** |
> |---|---|
> | **girl's** bike | **girls'** bikes |
> | **town's** park | **towns'** parks |

Rewrite each sentence. Replace the underlined words with a possessive.

1. <u>The yard of my friend</u> is big.

   _____

2. <u>The leaves of the plant</u> are green.

   _____

3. <u>The thorns on the roses</u> are sharp.

   _____

4. <u>The dog that belongs to Dave</u> plays in the park.

   _____

5. <u>The toy of the dog</u> is stuck in the bush.

   _____

6. I sit under <u>the branches of the tree</u>.

   _____

Name _____ Date _____

Possessive Nouns

A possessive shows ownership. Add an apostrophe and **s** to the end of a singular noun to form a possessive. For a plural noun that ends in **s**, add an apostrophe after the **s** to form a possessive.

Singular Possessive	**Plural Possessive**
Ella's quilt	**babies'** blankets
farm's strawberries	**pickers'** baskets

Rewrite each sentence. Replace the underlined words with a possessive.

1. The <u>gates of the aquarium</u> are open.

_____

2. I want to see the <u>habitat of the seals</u>.

_____

3. The <u>fin of the blue whale</u> is huge!

_____

4. Did you see the <u>eggs of the penguin</u>?

_____

5. The <u>tail of the fish</u> is beautiful.

_____

6. When is the <u>feeding time of the dolphins</u>?

_____

Name _____ Date _____

Present Tense Verbs

> Verbs are actions words. Present tense verbs tell about actions that are happening right now. For the present tense, add **-s** or **-es** if the subject of a sentence is singular. Do not add **-s** or **-es** if the subject is plural.
>
> **Singular Verb:** <u>He</u> **buys** a kite.
>
> **Plural Verb:** <u>They</u> **buy** a kite.

Choose the correct verb. Write it on the line.

1. We (visit, visits) the animal shelter. _____

2. All kinds of animals (live, lives) there. _____

3. A volunteer (take, takes) us on a tour. _____

4. Black and white cats (run, runs) in circles. _____

5. Puppies (chase, chases) tennis balls. _____

6. An older brown dog (lick, licks) my hand. _____

7. Everyone (play, plays) with the puppies. _____

8. My family (adopt, adopts) the brown dog. _____

Name _____ Date _____

Present Tense Verbs

> Verbs are actions words. Present tense verbs tell about actions that are happening right now. For the present tense, add **-s** or **-es** if the subject of a sentence is singular. Do not add **-s** or **-es** if the subject is plural.
> **Singular Verb:** <u>Mom</u> **reads** the newspaper.
> **Plural Verb:** <u>We</u> **read** books at bedtime.

Write the present tense form of the verb in the parentheses ( ).

1. We (see) bats outside at night. _____

2. My dad (know) a lot about bats. _____

3. He (tell) me all about these flying mammals. _____

4. Bats (see) in the dark. _____

5. The vampire bat (bite) with its tiny sharp teeth. _____

6. It (eat) blood! _____

7. Vampire bats (live) in caves. _____

8. My dad (say) they are not so scary. _____

Name _____ Date _____

Past Tense Verbs

> Past tense verbs tell about actions that already happened. Past tense verbs often end in **-ed**. This is true whether the subject is singular or plural.
>
> <u>Maisie</u> **jumped** rope.
>
> <u>We</u> all **jumped** rope.

Write the past tense form of the verb in the parentheses ( ).

1. Last winter, Mom (order) seeds for her vegetable garden.

   _____

2. Together, we (plant) the seeds in the spring.

   _____

3. I (water) the seeds every day. _____

4. I (watch) the seeds become vegetable plants.

   _____

5. The sun (warm) them. _____

6. We (pick) and ate vegetables all summer.

   _____

20   Conquer Grammar • Grade 2 • © Newmark Learning, LLC

Name _____ Date _____

Irregular Past Tense Verbs

Past tense verbs tell about actions that already happened. Past tense verbs that do not end in **-ed** are irregular. Some examples of verbs and their irregular past tense forms include **fall/fell**, **slide/slid**, **tell/told**, **take/took**.

Choose a past tense verb from the box to complete each sentence. Write it on the line.

take	told	slide	fell
fall	tell	took	slid

1. I _____ last week in the rain.

2. We _____ a walk in the park.

3. I _____ across the wet sidewalk.

4. I _____ my sister about it.

Rewrite each sentence with the past tense form of the underlined verb.

5. Many snowflakes <u>fall</u>.

_____

6. We <u>slide</u> down the hill.

_____

Conquer Grammar • Grade 2 • © Newmark Learning, LLC

Name _____ Date _____

Irregular Past Tense Verbs

Past tense verbs tell about actions that already happened. Past tense verbs that do not end in **-ed** are irregular. Some examples of verbs and their irregular past tense forms include **begin/began**, **hide/hid**, **throw/threw**, **dig/dug**, **grow/grew**, **see/saw**.

Choose a past tense verb from the box to complete each sentence. Write it on the line.

hid	throw	grew	dig
grow	hide	dug	threw

1. My kitten _____ big this year.

2. Today, I _____ a ball of yarn to him.

3. He _____ the yarn behind the couch.

4. He _____ it out a few hours later.

Rewrite each sentence with the past tense form of the underlined verb.

5. The exam <u>begin</u> at 9:00 a.m.

   _____

6. They <u>see</u> the movie.

   _____

Name _____ Date _____

Irregular Past Tense Verbs

> Past tense verbs tell about actions that already happened. Past tense verbs that do not end in **-ed** are irregular. Some examples of verbs and their irregular past tense forms include **get/got**, **do/did**, **ride/rode**, **buy/bought**, **ring/rang**.

Choose a past tense verb from the box to complete each sentence. Write it on the line.

rode	do	ring	got
get	rang	did	ride

1. The bell _____ at the end of class.

2. Sally _____ her bike around the block.

3. I _____ well on the spelling quiz.

4. Mom _____ a new shirt from the store.

Rewrite each sentence with the past tense form of the underlined verb.

5. They <u>ride</u> in the car.

_____

6. They <u>buy</u> groceries.

_____

Name _____ Date _____

Irregular Past Tense Verbs

> Past tense verbs tell about actions that already happened. Past tense verbs that do not end in **-ed** are irregular. Some examples of verbs and their irregular past tense forms include **send/sent**, **say/said**, **leave/left**, **wear/wore**, **grow/grew**, **see/saw**.

Choose the correct verb. Write it on the line.

1. I (leave, left) my jacket at home. _____

2. Mom (said, say) the weather was cold. _____

3. I wish I (wore, wear) my jacket. _____

4. Mom (send, sent) my jacket to school. _____

Rewrite each sentence using the past tense form of the underlined verb.

5. I <u>send</u> a letter.

_____

6. I <u>say</u> good morning.

_____

Name _____ Date _____

Future Tense Verbs

Future tense verbs tell about actions that will happen at a later time. To form the future tense, place the word **will** in front of the verb.

Gillian **will watch** her baby sister.

Mom **will bake** a cake.

Write the future tense form of the verb in the parentheses ( ).

1. Tara (win) the race. _____

2. She (practice) every day. _____

3. Dad (help) Tara stay focused. _____

4. He (be) her coach. _____

5. Tara (eat) healthfully to stay in shape. _____

6. She (buy) new sneakers. _____

7. Dad (pay) for them. _____

8. Tara (sleep) eight hours a night. _____

Name _____ Date _____

Future Tense Verbs

> Future tense verbs tell about actions that will happen at a later time. To form the future tense, place the word **will** in front of the verb.
>
> Hannah **will run** in the race.
> We **will cheer** for her.

Write the future tense form of the verb in the parentheses ( ).

1. Neil (play) hockey this winter. _____

2. He (need) lots of equipment. _____

3. Dad (take) him shopping. _____

4. They (shop) at the secondhand store. _____

Rewrite each sentence with the future tense form of the underlined verb.

5. The equipment <u>cost</u> much less there.

   _____

6. They <u>save</u> money and the environment.

   _____

Name _____ Date _____

Verb Tenses

> The tense of a verb tells when the action happens. To form the past tense of most verbs, add **ed**. For the present tense, use the verb alone or add an **s** or **-es**. To form the future tense, add the word **will** in front of the verb.
>
> **Past**
> Last year I **learned** to swim.
>
> **Present**
> Now, I **learn** to play baseball.
>
> **Future**
> Next year, I **will learn** to play tennis.

Read each sentence. Write *past*, *present*, or *future* for the underlined verb.

1. We keep a monarch butterfly in our classroom. _____

2. The butterfly started as an egg. _____

3. Then the egg hatched into a caterpillar. _____

4. We watched the caterpillar turn into a butterfly. _____

5. The black-and-orange butterfly lives in a cage. _____

Choose the correct verb. Write it on the line.

6. Tomorrow we (set, will set) the butterfly free. _____

7. It (flew, will fly) south for the winter. _____

Name _____ Date _____

Verb Tenses

The tense of a verb tells when the action happens. To form the past tense of most verbs, add **ed**. For the present tense, use the verb alone or add an **s** or **-es**. To form the future tense, add the word **will** in front of the verb.

Past	**Present**	**Future**
This morning, Mom **walked** the dog.	Now Dad and I **walk** him.	Tonight, Dad **will walk** him.

Choose the correct verb. Write it on the line.

1. Yesterday, I (lost, will lose) my baseball glove. _____

2. I (think, will think) I left it at the field. _____

3. After school today, Mom and I (looked, will look) for it. _____

4. I (hope, hoped) it is there. _____

5. It (was, will be) a birthday present. _____

Read each sentence. Write *past*, *present*, or *future* for the underlined verb.

6. We <u>searched</u> in the dugout. _____

7. I <u>found</u> the glove under the bench. _____

Name _____ Date _____

Collective Nouns with Matching Verbs

> A collective noun names a group of people, places, or things. A collective noun is singular even though it names more than one. Use singular verbs with collective nouns. A singular verb ends in **s**.
>
> Our **family** <u>eats</u> together.
>
> The **jury** <u>listens</u> to the judge.

Underline the collective noun in each sentence. Then rewrite the sentence with the correct form of the verb.

1. Our troop camp in the forest.

   _____

2. The forest come alive.

   _____

3. A flock of birds sing in the tree.

   _____

4. A herd of deer run in the meadow.

   _____

5. A school of fish swim in the lake.

   _____

Name _____ Date _____

Singular and Plural Nouns with Matching Verbs

> In a sentence, the noun, or subject, and the verb must match. A singular noun takes a singular verb. A plural noun takes a plural verb.
>
> The <u>rabbit</u> **hops**.
>
> The three <u>rabbits</u> **hop**.

Choose the correct verb. Write it on the line.

1. The spider _____ a web.   (spin, spins)

2. The ants _____ on the log.   (crawl, crawls)

3. The bees _____ in the field.   (buzz, buzzes)

4. The butterfly _____ its wings.   (spread, spreads)

5. The worms _____ through the dirt.   (slide, slides)

Read each sentence. Choose the correct verb in the parentheses ( ). Write it on the line.

6. Frogs (jump, jumps) high. _____

7. The bird (sing, sings) a song. _____

Name _____ Date _____

Personal Pronouns

Pronouns are words that take the place of nouns.
I, **me**, **you**, **he**, **him**, **she**, **her**, **it**, **we**, **us**, **you**, **they**, and **them** are personal pronouns. They are used to refer to a specific person or thing, and to avoid repetition of the noun.

Noun	**Personal Pronoun**
Julio got his own key.	**He** got his own key.
Julio put the **key** on a key chain.	Julio put **it** on a key chain.

Choose a personal pronoun from the box to complete each sentence. Write it on the line.

he	him	it	they	them

1. Mom bought a violin for _____.

2. _____ put the violin in a safe place.

3. His friends Billy and Eric asked to see _____.

4. _____ were so excited!

5. Julio asked _____ to be careful.

6. Julio did not want to break _____.

Name _____ Date _____

Personal Pronouns

> Pronouns are words that take the place of nouns.
> **I**, **me**, **you**, **he**, **him**, **she**, **her**, **it**, **we**, **us**, **you**, **they**, and **them** are personal pronouns. They are used to refer to a specific person or thing, and to avoid repetition of the noun.
>
> | **Noun** | **Personal Pronoun** |
> |---|---|
> | **Kara** buys a bike. | **She** buys a bike. |
> | **Kara** rides the bike before **Kara** buys it. | **Kara** rides the bike before **she** buys it. |

Write the personal pronoun *he, she, him, her, it, they,* or *them* for the underlined word or words.

1. <u>Kara and Dad</u> went for a bike ride. _____

2. <u>Kara</u> got a flat tire. _____

3. The flat made <u>Kara and Dad</u> stop. _____

4. <u>Dad</u> had a pump and a patch. _____

5. Dad helped <u>Kara</u> fix the flat tire. _____

6. <u>The tire</u> was good as new. _____

7. Kara thanked <u>Dad</u> and they kept riding. _____

8. <u>Kara and Dad</u> finished the bike trail. _____

Name _____ Date _____

Possessive Pronouns

Pronouns take the place of nouns. Possessive pronouns tell who or what owns something. **My**, **mine**, **our**, **ours**, **its**, **his**, **her**, **hers**, **their**, **theirs**, **your**, and **yours** are possessive pronouns.
   The bird built a nest in **Fiona's** tree.
   The bird built a nest in **her** tree.
   The bird cleaned **the bird's** feathers.
   The bird cleaned **its** feathers.

Read each sentence. Underline the possessive pronoun.

1. The bird used twigs to build its nest.

2. I can see the nest from our bathroom window.

3. My whole family watches the bird's nest.

4. We use our binoculars to see better.

Write the correct possessive pronoun for the underlined word or words.

5. Fiona thinks the nest is Fiona's. _____

6. That is because it is in Fiona's tree. _____

7. I bet the bird thinks it is the bird's nest. _____

Name _____ Date _____

Possessive Pronouns

Pronouns take the place of nouns. Possessive pronouns tell who or what owns something. **My**, **mine**, **our**, **ours**, **its**, **his**, **her**, **hers, their**, **theirs**, **your**, and **yours** are possessive pronouns.
  We call **Mom's** parents Nana and Poppy.
  We call **her** parents Nana and Poppy.
  We call **Dad's** parents Grandma and Grandpa.
  We call **his** parents Grandma and Grandpa.

Choose a personal pronoun from the box to complete each sentence. Write it on the line.

| her | their | our | his | theirs | my |

1. I packed _____ suitcase last night.

2. My brothers packed _____ also.

3. We are going to visit _____ grandparents.

4. Mom will be happy to see _____ parents.

5. Dad calls them _____ second parents.

6. We will stay at _____ house for a week.

Name _____ Date _____

Indefinite Pronouns

Pronouns are words that take the place of nouns. Indefinite pronouns don't refer to a specific person or thing.
There was **nothing** left to eat.
Everybody went home.

Read each sentence. Underline the indefinite pronoun.

1. Somebody spilled a glass of milk.

2. Everybody's milk spilled.

3. Nobody knew who did it.

4. Everybody pointed at the cat.

5. The cat could not say anything.

Choose the correct indefinite pronoun.
Write it on the line.

6. (Nobody, Nothing) wanted to clean the mess.

   _____

7. Mom said (anything, everyone) should help clean up.

   _____

Name _____ Date _____

Indefinite Pronouns

Pronouns are words that take the place of nouns. Indefinite pronouns don't refer to a specific person or thing.
   Did **anyone** lose money?
   Someone found two dollars in the cafeteria.

Choose an indefinite pronoun from the box to complete each sentence. Write it on the line.

| anybody | anything | everyone | somewhere | nobody |

1. This road must lead _____.

2. Do you have _____ to say?

3. We need a bus that will fit _____.

4. The phone kept ringing because _____ was home.

5. _____ can find my baseball glove.

6. Does _____ have a pencil I can borrow?

7. The stadium was empty because there was _____ at the game.

Name _____   Date _____

Reflexive Pronouns

> Pronouns are words that take the place of nouns. Reflexive pronouns refer back to the subject and always end in **-self** or **-selves**. **Myself, yourself, himself, herself, itself, ourselves, yourselves,** and **themselves** are reflexive pronouns.
>
> The cat saved **the cat** from the fire.
> The cat saved **itself** from the fire.
> My cousins take care of **my cousins**.
> My cousins take care of **themselves**.

Read each sentence. Underline the reflexive pronoun.

1. She hurt herself when she fell.

2. We blame ourselves for the low attendance of the event.

3. My little brother can feed himself.

4. You can help yourself to more food.

Read each sentence. Write *themselves, himself,* or *herself* for the underlined word or words.

5. Lisa wrote <u>Lisa</u> a note. _____

6. The students lined <u>the students</u> up for lunch. _____

7. My grandfather taught <u>my grandfather</u> to read. _____

Name _____ Date _____

Reflexive Pronouns

> Pronouns are words that take the place of nouns. Reflexive pronouns refer back to the subject and always end in **-self** or **-selves**. **Myself, yourself, himself, herself, itself, ourselves, yourselves,** and **themselves** are reflexive pronouns.
>
> Ricky bought **Ricky** a new camera.
> Ricky bought **himself** a new camera.
> The teammates took a picture of the **teammates**.
> The teammates took a picture of **themselves**.

From the box, choose the possessive pronoun that best completes each sentence. Write it on the line.

| herself | myself | itself | ourselves | himself | themselves |

1. I saw _____ in the mirror.

2. My baby brother sings to _____.

3. Our cat spends hours grooming _____.

4. The students were proud of _____.

5. Mom poured _____ a cup of coffee.

6. We read to _____ during independent time.

Name _____ Date _____

Adjectives

> Adjectives are words that describe nouns, adjectives, or adverbs. Adjectives give details about people, places, and things. They tell about size, color, number, and kind. In the phrase *the blue rug*, the adjective **blue** tells the color of the noun **rug**.

Read each sentence. Circle the adjective and underline the noun it describes.

1. Jasmine refused to clean her messy room.

2. She was looking for her orange backpack.

3. Anya enjoys cooking delicious food.

4. He dislikes washing dirty dishes.

5. Bryn thinks that the park is small.

6. That annoying alarm clock keeps buzzing!

7. Luis's youngest brother misbehaves.

8. Dan's older cousin is nice.

9. The town has a lot of pretty houses.

10. The theater has a big stage.

Name _____ Date _____

Adjectives

> Adjectives are words that describe nouns, adjectives, or adverbs. Adjectives give details about people, places, and things. They tell about size, color, number, and kind. In the phrase *the brown dog*, the adjective **brown** tells the color of the noun **dog**.

Read each sentence. Underline the adjective and circle the noun it describes.

1. Nicole wore red shoes to the party.

2. Max bakes delicious cakes.

3. We were excited to see our old friends.

4. Elena planted purple flowers.

5. Mike draws beautiful pictures.

6. Andrew collects old stamps.

7. My cat doesn't like loud noises.

8. Liam played beautiful music.

Name _____ Date _____

Adjectives

Adjectives are words that describe nouns, adjectives, or adverbs. Adjectives give details about people, places, and things. They tell about size, color, number, and kind. In the sentence *Olga gave me two flowers*, the adjective **two** tells the number of the noun **flowers**.

Read each sentence. Underline the adjective and circle the noun it describes.

1. I am a talented artist.

2. I like to paint big pictures.

3. I want to paint this sunny park.

4. I like to draw with my red marker.

5. Will you take one picture with me?

6. I need a white dress.

7. I love rainy weather.

8. Luca bought green apples.

Name _____   Date _____

Adjectives

> Adjectives are words that describe nouns, adjectives, or adverbs. Adjectives give details about people, places, and things. They tell about size, color, number, and kind. In the phrase *the slippery stones*, the adjective **slippery** tells the kind of **stones**.

Read each sentence. Underline the adjective and circle the noun it describes.

1. Carlos has two sisters.

2. Everyone enjoyed the delicious meal.

3. We woke up to a cloudy sky.

4. A giant tree blocked the trail.

Choose an adjective from the box to complete each sentence. Write it on the line.

| green | deep | small | two |

5. The _____ kitten started to purr.

6. Eliza checks out _____ library books.

7. Ted wore a _____ sweater.

8. After the storm, we splashed in the _____ puddles.

Name _____ Date _____

Adverbs

> Adverbs describe verbs, nouns, adjectives, and adverbs. They give details about how, when, or where an action happens. Other examples of adverbs include **before**, **here**, **later**, and **there**.
>
> We sing **loudly**. We sang this song **before**.
> We stand **here**. Our teacher stands **nearby**.

Read each sentence. Circle the verb and underline the adverb.

1. We visited the lake yesterday.

2. The children played quietly.

3. The turtles moved slowly.

4. We fed bread to the ducks later.

5. Dad swam nearby.

Underline the adverb in each sentence. Then circle whether the adverb tells how, when, or where.

6. I always brush my teeth.
    How   When   Where

7. Let's eat there!
    How   When   Where

Name _____ Date _____

Adverbs

> Adverbs describe verbs, nouns, adjectives, and adverbs. They give details about how, when, or where an action happens.
>
> We spoke **clearly**. We recited the poem **before**.
> I left my book **somewhere**. James **eagerly** stood up.

Read each sentence. Circle the verb and underline the adverb.

1. I happily volunteered to help shovel the snow.

2. The workers drove to the office daily.

3. We held the presentation outdoors.

4. We all performed beautifully.

5. We threw a party afterward.

Underline the adverb in each sentence. Then circle whether the adverb tells who, when, or where.

6. Weeds grow everywhere.   How   When   Where

7. Amanda carefully pulls them.   How   When   Where

8. Tomato plants will sprout soon.   How   When   Where

Name _____ Date _____

Adjectives and Adverbs

> Adjectives describe nouns, adjectives, and adverbs. Adverbs describe verbs, nouns, adjectives, and adverbs.
>
> **Adjective:** My new shoes are **perfect**!
>
> **Adverb:** My new shoes fit **perfectly**!

Choose the adjective or the adverb. Write it on the line.

1. The _____ flight took only an hour.

   (shortly   short)

2. Juan _____ waited for the show to start.

   (excitedly   exciting)

3. I rode my scooter _____.

   (quickly   quick)

4. Jen _____ helped Max with his homework.

   (happily   happy)

5. We went to the theater to hear _____ music.

   (beautifully   beautiful)

Conquer Grammar • Grade 2 • © Newmark Learning, LLC

Name _____ Date _____

Adjectives and Adverbs

> Adjectives describe nouns, adjectives, and adverbs. Adverbs describe verbs, nouns, adjectives, and adverbs.
> **Adjective:** The **brave** firefighters put out the fire.
> **Adverb:** The firefighters **bravely** put out the fire.

Choose the correct adjective or adverb from the box to complete each sentence. Write it on the line.

strange	strangely	happy	loudly
happily	loud	sweet	sweetly

1. Nick picked up the _____ object to take a closer look.

2. This cake is _____.

3. I sang _____ to the music.

4. I ran _____ toward the park.

5. My winter jacket fit _____ after I grew.

6. The marching band was so _____!

7. My sister was _____ to knit me a new sweater.

Name _____ Date _____

Comparatives and Superlatives

Use comparative adjectives and adverbs to compare two people, places, or things. Add **-er** to most one-syllable adjectives and adverbs to compare two. Add **-est** to form the superlative to compare more than two.

Adjectives
My turtle is **smaller** than my gerbil.

My fish is the **smallest** of all.

Adverbs
Buddy runs **faster** than Rusty.

The black dog runs the **fastest** of all.

Underline the comparative or superlative adjective or adverb in each sentence. Then circle whether it compares two or more than two.

1. Jen arrived sooner than Scott.   two   more than two

2. Angelo studied harder than I did.   two   more than two

3. She is the smartest person I know.   two   more than two

Choose the comparative adjective or the comparative adverb. Write it on the line.

4. The weather is _____ today than yesterday. (colder, coldest)

5. My kite flew _____ than Evan's kite. (higher, highest)

Name _____   Date _____

Comparatives and Superlatives

Comparatives compare two or more people, places, or things. Superlatives compare three or more. For an adjective or adverb that has more than one syllable and does not end in **y**, place the word **more** or **most** in front of the word to make the comparative. **More** compares two things and **most** compares more than two things.

Adjectives

Our porch is **more peaceful** than the living room.

My room is the **most peaceful** place of all.

Adverbs

Ava rides **more carefully** than Oliver.

Frankie rides **most carefully** of all.

Underline the comparative or superlative in each sentence. Then circle whether it compares two or more than two.

1. My sister dances more gracefully than I do.

   two   more than two

2. Carly is the most talented singer in the choir.

   two   more than two

3. Mr. Bruno is the most skillful art teacher.

   two   more than two

4. Of all our neighbors, our family hosts parties most often.

   two   more than two

Name _____ Date _____

Comparatives and Superlatives

> Add **-er** to most one-syllable adjectives and adverbs to compare two (comparative). Add **-est** to most one-syllable adjectives and adverbs to compare more than two (superlative). If an adjective or adverb has more than one syllable and does not end in **y**, use **more** to compare two things and **most** to compare more than two things.
>
> **Compare Two**
> We took the **shorter** of the two trails.
>
> I walked **slower** than Liam.
>
> This trail is **more rugged** than the last.
>
> **Compare More than Two**
> The east trail is the **longest** of all.
>
> Karen walked the **fastest**.
>
> Which trail is the **most scenic**?

Underline the comparative or superlative adjective or adverb. Circle whether it compares two or more than two.

1. Carlos worked harder than I did.

　　two　　more than two

2. His pastries were better than mine.

　　two　　more than two

3. The most talented chef won the contest.

　　two　　more than two

4. Snowboarding seems more difficult than skiing.

　　two　　more than two

Name _____ Date _____

Prepositions

> Prepositions connect two or more words in a sentence and show how they are related. Some prepositions show where something is. Others show where or when something happens.
>
> This book belongs **in** the library.
> The next game is **on** Saturday.

Circle the preposition in each sentence.

1. Aldo poured milk on his cereal.

2. We went to the movies.

3. The visitor left after lunch.

4. The vines grew up the wall.

5. Nadia looked at the painting.

6. The dog climbed over the fence.

7. I cheered during the game.

8. My house is by the school.

Name _____ Date _____

Conjunctions

> Use conjunctions such as **and**, **or**, **but**, **so**, or **because** to combine shorter sentences.
>
>   I play soccer. I play baseball.
>
>   I play soccer **and** baseball.

Combine each pair of sentences using the conjunction in the parentheses ( ). Write the new sentence on the line.

1. I ate an apple. I ate a pear. (and)

   _____

2. We may go today. We may go tomorrow. (or)

   _____

3. Would you like milk? Would you like juice? (or)

   _____

4. Yesterday was cold. It was sunny. (but)

   _____

5. The game ended. We went home. (so)

   _____

6. I went to sleep. I was tired. (because)

   _____

Name _____   Date _____

Articles

> The words **a**, **an**, and **the** are articles. Use **the** to tell about an exact person, place, or thing. Use **a** or **an** to tell about any person, place, or thing. Use **a** before a consonant sound and **an** before a vowel sound.
>
> Dad went to **the** store.
> He wanted to buy **an** umbrella.
> It was **a** rainy day.

Choose the correct article. Write it on the line.

1. Lena went to (a, the) kitchen. _____

2. She opened (an, the) refrigerator. _____

3. She grabbed (a, an) apple. _____

4. She got (a, the) peanut butter. _____

5. Then she looked for (a, the) plate. _____

6. She could only find (a, the) bowl. _____

7. She sat down at (a, the) table. _____

8. She ate (a, the) sandwich. _____

Name _____ Date _____

Demonstratives

> **This**, **that**, **these**, and **those** are demonstratives.
> Demonstratives tell about specific people, places, or things.
> Use **this** and **these** to talk about things that are nearby.
> Use **that** and **those** to talk about things that are far away.
> Use **this** and **that** with singular nouns, and **these** and **those** with plural nouns.
>
> **This** is my desk.
> **That** locker is mine.
> **These** markers go in my desk.
> **Those** markers belong to Ricky.

Choose the correct demonstrative. Write it on the line.

1. (This, These) is the block where I live. _____

2. (This, Those) are my neighbors across the street.
 _____

3. (This, These) is my house. _____

4. (That, Those) is my mom's car in the driveway.
 _____

5. (Those, These) are my house keys. _____

6. (That, This) is my cat in the upstairs window. _____

Name _____   Date _____

Commas in Series

> Use commas to separate three or more words in a series.
> Ivan grows lettuce, tomatoes, and cucumbers.

Read each sentence. Write commas where needed.

1. We walk skip and run in gym class.

2. Marco Adam and Shawn play hockey.

3. The puppy has brown gray and white fur.

4. We had salad chicken and rice for dinner.

5. Dad bought cereal chips and fruit at the store.

Rewrite each sentence with the correct punctuation.

6. Mrs. Dooley visited Arizona Nevada and New Mexico.

   _____

7. She traveled by car train and plane.

   _____

8. Theo James and Yoko play guitar.

   _____

Name _____ Date _____

Commas in Dates and Series

> Use commas in dates, and to separate three or more words in a series.
>
> The school opened on Monday, October 6, 1980.
> Ariel likes to sing, dance, and act.

Read each sentence. Write commas where needed.

1. My sister plays basketball soccer and softball.

2. I found an old newspaper dated Saturday March 3 1934.

3. Mom grows pink purple and yellow flowers.

Rewrite each sentence with the correct punctuation.

4. The triplets are named Luke Matt and Daniel.

_____

5. They were born on Tuesday November 16 2010.

_____

6. Vivian wore a hat mittens and a scarf.

_____

Conquer Grammar • Grade 2 • © Newmark Learning, LLC

Name _____ Date _____

Commas in Introductory Phrases and Clauses

> A comma (,) is used to set off an introductory phrase or clause in a sentence.
>
> Later in the day, we will visit the museum.
> Once we were on our way, we were fine.

Read each sentence. Write commas where needed.

1. Before we went shopping Mom clipped coupons.

2. When the rain started we ran inside the house.

3. While we were in the park I saw three squirrels.

4. After jumping in a puddle Nina had to dry off.

5. To prepare for the picnic we made some lemonade.

Rewrite each sentence with the correct punctuation.

6. Before Sara left the party she said good-bye to everyone.

_____

7. While we are watching the movie let's eat our snacks.

_____

Commas in Greetings

> Letters or e-mails begin with a greeting. A greeting consists of a word such as **Dear** or **Hi** and the name of the person to whom you are writing, followed by a comma. Every word in a greeting should begin with a capital letter.
>
> **Dear** Mrs. Grant**,**   **Hi** Carlos**,**   **Dear** Diary**,**

Read each greeting. Write a comma where needed.

1. Dear Tony
   Will you come to my party?

2. Dear Diary
   I rode my scooter to school.

3. Hi Kelsey
   Meet me at the mall.

4. Dear Evan
   Did you find your gear?

5. Hi Uncle Mike
   How are you?

6. Hi Grandma
   I miss you.

Rewrite the letter opening correctly on the lines.

Dear Andy Thank you for the gift.

_____

_____

Name _____ Date _____

Commas in Closings

> Letters or e-mails end with a closing. A closing consists of a word or words such as **Yours**, **Yours truly**, **Love**, or **Sincerely** followed by a comma. The author's name should appear below the closing. Only the first word in a closing should begin with a capital letter.
>
> **Yours truly,**   **Love,**   **Sincerely,**
> Antonio   Mom and Dad   Mrs. Kim

Circle whether each phrase is a greeting or a closing. Then rewrite it correctly on the line.

1. Your friend _____ greeting   closing

2. Dear Carmen _____ greeting   closing

3. Hi Roger _____ greeting   closing

4. With love _____ greeting   closing

5. Yours truly _____ greeting   closing

Rewrite the letter closing correctly on the lines.

Your friend Marco

_____

_____

58   Conquer Grammar • Grade 2 • © Newmark Learning, LLC

Name _____ Date _____

Commas in Greetings and Closings

Letters or e-mails begin with a greeting and end with a closing. Greetings and closings are always followed by a comma.

Dear Cole**,**
I had fun at your party.
Your pal,
Inez

Hi Kate**,**
We won the game!
Yours joyfully,
Brian

Rewrite each greeting or closing correctly on the line.

1. hi john

_____

2. your pal

_____

3. dear aunt mary

_____

4. best wishes

_____

5. dear sister

_____

6. until then

_____

Form a closing by writing the words in the correct order. Remember to add a comma.

son   your   loving

_____

Conquer Grammar • Grade 2 • © Newmark Learning, LLC

Name _____ Date _____

Commas in Greetings and Closings

> Letters or e-mails begin with a greeting and end with a closing. Greetings and closings are always followed by a comma.
>
> **Dear** Mayor Brown**,**
> Please consider my plan
> for the new park.
> **Sincerely,**
> Mrs. Palmer
>
> **Hi** Amir**,**
> I miss you so much!
> **Love,**
> Kiki

Circle whether each phrase is a greeting or a closing. Then rewrite it correctly on the line.

1. Hi Tina _____   greeting   closing

2. All my best _____   greeting   closing

3. Dear Diary _____   greeting   closing

4. Your friend _____   greeting   closing

5. With love _____   greeting   closing

Form a greeting by writing the words in the correct order. Remember to add a comma.

Sue   Aunt   Dear

_____

Name _____ Date _____

End Marks

> An end mark is the punctuation that comes at the end of a sentence.
>
> Statements or telling sentences end in a period: **.**
>
> Sentences that ask a question end in question mark: **?**
>
> Sentences that show strong feeling end in an exclamation mark: **!**
>
> Sentences that give commands usually end in a period: **.**

Read each sentence. Write the correct end mark.

1. I love amusement parks _____

2. We visit one every summer _____

3. This summer we will go to Lake Compounce _____

4. Have you ever been there _____

5. Come with us _____

6. We are leaving tomorrow _____

End Marks

An end mark is the punctuation that comes at the end of a sentence.

Statements or telling sentences end in a period: **.**

Sentences that ask a question end in question mark: **?**

Sentences that show strong feeling end in an exclamation mark: **!**

Sentences that give commands end in a period: **.** or an exclamation mark: **!**

Read each sentence. Write the correct end mark.

1. I know lots about sharks _____

2. The shark has thousands of sharp teeth _____

3. The shark's eyes look a lot like ours _____

4. Sharks were here even before the dinosaurs _____

5. I would love to see a shark one day _____

6. Do you want to learn about sharks _____

7. I have some books you can borrow _____

Name _____ Date _____

Contractions

A contraction is a shortened form of a word or words. An apostrophe (') replaces the dropped letter or letters in a contraction.

Words	Contraction
will not	won't
I have	I've
could not	couldn't
does not	doesn't

Choose a contraction from the box to take the place of the underlined words in each sentence. Write the contraction on the line.

I've	couldn't	didn't
won't	she'd	wasn't

1. Robert <u>was not</u> at the show. _____

2. He <u>could not</u> get a ticket. _____

3. He <u>did not</u> want to stay home. _____

4. <u>I have</u> asked him to come over. _____

5. He <u>will not</u> come alone. _____

6. He said <u>she would</u> bring a friend. _____

Name _____   Date _____

Contractions

> A contraction is a shortened form of a word or words. An apostrophe replaces the dropped letter or letters in a contraction.
>
> **I will** go to the party.   **I'll** go to the party.

Underline the contraction in each sentence. Then write the words that make the contraction.

1. Let's meet before the movie starts. _____

2. Doesn't the rain get in the way of the parade? _____

3. I guess we'll see Ava when we get there. _____

4. I don't like the heat. _____

5. It isn't fair that we have to stay inside! _____

6. Olivia didn't get my letter, so I will resend it. _____

7. Zeke is not able to go to the store today, so he'll go tomorrow. _____

8. Mom said they're almost here! _____

Name _____ Date _____

Contractions

> A contraction is a shortened form of a word or words. An apostrophe (') replaces the dropped letter or letters in a contraction.
>
> | Words | Contraction |
> |---|---|
> | do not | don't |
> | cannot | can't |
> | has not | hasn't |

Underline the contraction in each sentence. Then write the word or words that make the contraction.

1. I've never been to the carnival. _____

2. Maddie hasn't bought the book yet. _____

3. Jenna can't find her cat. _____

4. Who'll be coming to the bake sale? _____

5. Don't forget to let the dog out. _____

Rewrite each sentence. Replace the underlined words with a contraction.

6. The catcher <u>did not</u> come to the softball game.

_____

7. Amanda <u>could not</u> bring her brother to school.

_____

Name _____ Date _____

Contractions

> A contraction is a shortened form of a word or words. An apostrophe (') replaces the dropped letter or letters in a contraction.
>
> | Words | Contraction |
> |---|---|
> | does not | doesn't |
> | who will | who'll |
> | we have | we've |
> | are not | aren't |

Underline the contraction in each sentence. Then write the words that make the contraction.

1. Nick hasn't read the book. _____

2. Nadia doesn't have an extra copy. _____

3. Who'll lend Nick the book? _____

4. We've seen plenty of copies in the library. _____

Rewrite each sentence. Replace the underlined words with a contraction.

5. The books are not on the table.

    _____

6. Tito is not here yet.

    _____

Name _____ Date _____

Contractions

A contraction is a shortened form of a word or words. An apostrophe (') replaces the dropped letter or letters in a contraction.

Words	Contraction
did not	didn't
who is	who's
I have	I've
I will	I'll
we are	we're

Underline each contraction. On the line, write the two words that form it.

1. The team didn't play very well. _____

2. We weren't impressed by their teamwork. _____

3. Who's going to the carnival next week? _____

4. I've already bought my tickets. _____

Rewrite each sentence. Replace the underlined words with a contraction.

5. I will see you at the theater!

_____

6. We are getting there early.

_____

Conquer Grammar • Grade 2 • © Newmark Learning, LLC

Name _____ Date _____

Contractions and Possessive Nouns

> A contraction is a shortened form of a word or words. An apostrophe replaces the dropped letter or letters in a contraction. Possessive nouns show that a person, place, or thing has or owns something. Add an apostrophe (') and an **s** to make a singular possessive noun.
>
> **Contraction**   **Possessive**
>
> **Emma's** my best friend.   **Emma's sweater** is red.

For each sentence, circle whether the underlined word is a contraction or a possessive.

1. Is <u>Kyra's</u> birthday next week?   Contraction   Possessive

2. <u>Let's</u> throw a surprise party!   Contraction   Possessive

3. <u>She'll</u> be happy.   Contraction   Possessive

4. Jack has her <u>friends'</u> addresses.   Contraction   Possessive

Rewrite each sentence. Replace the underlined words with a contraction or a possessive.

5. The party is at <u>the house belonging to Brendan</u>.

   _____

6. Please <u>do not</u> come late.

   _____

Name _____ Date _____

Contractions and Possessive Nouns

A contraction is a shortened form of a word or words. An apostrophe replaces the dropped letter or letters in a contraction. Possessive nouns show that a person, place, or thing has or owns something. Add an apostrophe (') and an **s** to make a singular possessive noun.

Contraction

Let's go to the store.

Possessive

Jason's friend wants a new belt.

Rewrite each sentence. Replace the underlined words with a contraction.

1. <u>I am</u> looking for red pants. _____

2. <u>She is</u> going to buy jeans. _____

3. <u>Where is</u> the closest store? _____

Rewrite each sentence. Replace the underlined words with a possessive.

4. <u>The shoe size of Michelle</u> is smaller than mine.

_____

5. <u>The manager of the store</u> was helpful.

_____

Capitalize Titles and Names, Days, and Months

A proper noun names a specific person, place, or thing. Each main word in a proper noun should begin with a capital letter. The titles and names of people, the days of the week, and the months of the year are proper nouns.

Title and Name	**Day**	**Month**
Ms. Olivia Trent	Sunday	January

Circle the proper noun in each sentence. Then write it correctly on the line.

1. Our principal's name is ms. lana gomez. _____

2. Have you met officer kevin paul? _____

3. I have an appointment with my dentist, dr. don costa.

   _____

Circle whether each proper noun names a day or a month. Then write it correctly on the line.

4. wednesday _____   Day   Month

5. july _____   Day   Month

6. november _____   Day   Month

Name _____ Date _____

Capitalize Geographic Names

Geographic names of specific places are proper nouns. Each main word in a proper noun should begin with a capital letter.

Geographic Names
Brooklyn Bridge
North Carolina
San Francisco

Circle the geographic name in each sentence. Then write it correctly on the line.

1. I am going on a trip to greenville. _____

2. It is a city in the state of south carolina. _____

3. I went camping in yosemite national park.
   _____

4. The park is in california. _____

5. There are many musicals to see in new york city.
   _____

6. The capital city is albany. _____

7. Someday, I want to visit france. _____

Conquer Grammar • Grade 2 • © Newmark Learning, LLC

Name _____ Date _____

Capitalize Geographic Names

> Geographic names of specific places are proper nouns. Each main word in a proper noun should begin with a capital letter.
>
> **Geographic Names**
> Great Bear Lake
> Canada
> Mount Rushmore

Circle the geographic name in each sentence. Then write it correctly on the line.

1. I live in chicago. _____

2. They lived in alabama. _____

Rewrite each sentence with correct capitalization.

3. I went to oregon. _____

4. I saw the pacific ocean. _____

5. We stopped in portland. _____

6. We visited cannon beach. _____

Name _____ Date _____

Capitalize Holidays

> The names of specific holidays are proper nouns. Each main word in a proper noun should begin with a capital letter.
>
> **Holidays**
> Labor Day
> New Year's Eve

**Circle the holiday name in each sentence.
Then write it correctly on the line.**

1. School is closed on new year's day.

   _____

2. Is st. patrick's day your favorite holiday?

   _____

3. We planted a tree on earth day.

   _____

4. What do you do on labor day?

   _____

5. I watched fireworks on independence day.

   _____

6. We visit Max on thanksgiving.

   _____

Name _____ Date _____

Capitalize Geographic Names and Holidays

> Geographic names of specific places and names of specific holidays are proper nouns. Each main word of a proper noun should begin with a capital letter.
>
> | **Geographic Names** | **Holidays** |
> |---|---|
> | Rocky Mountains | Independence Day |
> | Mississippi River | Labor Day |

Underline the geographic name in each sentence. Then write the sentence correctly on the line.

1. I live on main street. _____

2. Aaron lives near lake erie. _____

3. Ana took a trip to spain. _____

Underline the holiday in each sentence. Then write the sentence with the correct capitalization.

4. We handed out apples on halloween.

_____

5. School is closed for veterans day.

_____

6. Manny planted a tree on arbor day.

_____

Name _____ Date _____

Sentence Types

> There are four different types of sentences.
>
> **Declarative:** statement or telling sentence — ends in a period **.**
>
> **Interrogative:** sentence that asks a question — ends in a question mark **?**
>
> **Exclamatory:** sentence that shows strong feeling — ends in an exclamation mark **!**
>
> **Imperative:** sentences that give commands — end in either a period **.** or an exclamation mark **!**

Rewrite each sentence with the correct punctuation.

1. The four seasons are fall, winter, spring, and summer

   _____

2. I like winter best

   _____

3. I like to ice skate, sled, and build snowmen

   _____

4. Do you have a favorite season

   _____

Name _____   Date _____

Sentence Types

> There are four different types of sentences.
>
> **Declarative:** statement or telling sentence — ends in a period .
>
> **Interrogative:** sentence that asks a question — ends in a question mark ?
>
> **Exclamatory:** sentence that shows strong feeling — ends in an exclamation mark !
>
> **Imperative:** sentences that give commands — end in either a period . or an exclamation mark !

Write a sentence to answer each question.

1. Where do you live?

   _____

2. What is your favorite food?

   _____

3. What do you do to relax?

   _____

4. What do you like best about school?

   _____

Name _____   Date _____

Simple Sentences

A sentence tells a complete thought. A simple sentence has a subject that tells who or what does something and a verb or action word that tells what the subject does.

| **Sentence** | **Who or What?** | **Does What?** |
| Aunt Jen makes bread. | Aunt Jen | makes bread |

Read each sentence. Underline the subject, or who or what does something. Circle what the subject does.

1. Ross and Carlos visit the zoo.

2. Ross looks at the penguins.

3. Carlos likes the elephants.

4. The snowflakes fell softly.

Put the words together to make a complete simple sentence. Write it on the line.

5. ate lunch.   The students

_____

6. Aaron   drank water.

_____

7. ran the bases.   Emma and Ned

_____

Simple Sentences

A sentence tells a complete thought. A simple sentence has a subject that tells who or what does something and a verb or action word that tells what the subject does.

Sentence	Who or What?	Does What?
My family went on a picnic.	My family	went on a picnic
My cousins and I played catch.	My cousins and I	played catch

Read each sentence. Underline the subject, or who or what does something. Circle what the subject does.

1. Tall trees shaded our picnic table.

2. Anna and I unpacked the lunch.

3. Aunt Lucy's salad had walnuts and carrots.

Put the words together to make a complete simple sentence. Write it on the line.

4. walked the dog   My cousin

_____

5. Uncle Rick   drank his coffee

_____

Name _____ Date _____

Simple Sentences

A simple sentence is made up of a complete thought with a subject, that tells who or what does something, and a verb or action word that tells what the subject does.

Sentence	Who or What?	Does What?
Dan throws a ball.	Dan	throws a ball
Will Sparky fetch the ball?	Sparky	fetch the ball

Put the words together to make a complete simple sentence. Write it on the line.

1. The boys   bike to the library.

_____

2. rides the bus.   Chris

_____

3. stop?   Will the bus

_____

4. Chris   runs fast!

_____

5. bus driver!   Stop,

_____

Name _____ Date _____

Compound Sentences

> A compound sentence is made up of two simple sentences that are joined by a comma and a conjunction, such as **and**, **but**, **or**, or **so**.
>
> I live in the desert. I like to hike.
>
> I live in the desert**,** **and** I like to hike.

Read each compound sentence. Circle the conjunction. Then write the two simple sentences that make up the compound sentence.

1. The park is crowded, but we have fun.

   _____   _____

2. We go down the slide, and we play on the swings.

   _____   _____

3. I find flowers, and Jess sees a puppy.

   _____   _____

4. It is time to go, but we will be back.

   _____   _____

5. I want to go skiing, but I hurt my knee.

   _____   _____

Name _____ Date _____

Compound Sentences

> A compound sentence is made up of two simple sentences that are joined by a comma and a conjunction, such as **and**, **but**, **or**, or **so**.
>
> I like music. I like to read.
>
> I like music**, and** I like to read.

Read each compound sentence. Circle the conjunction. Underline the two simple sentences.

1. Ryan lost his backpack, and José found it.

2. Kayla likes nonfiction, but Daniel likes folktales.

3. I will meet you at the park, or I will see you later.

Combine each pair of simple sentences to make a compound sentence. Add a comma and the conjunction *and* or *but*. Write the compound sentence on the line.

4. Blake called on the phone.   I answered.

_____

5. We got on our bikes.   We rode to the store.

_____

6. She got some crackers.   I bought cheese.

_____

Name _____ Date _____

Compound Sentences

> A compound sentence is made up of two simple sentences that are joined by a comma and a conjunction, such as **and**, **but**, **or**, or **so**.
>
> Mom bought a new vase. It was too small.
>
> Mom bought a new vase**,** **but** it was too small.

Combine each pair of simple sentences to make a compound sentence. Add a comma and the conjunction *and* **or** *but*. **Write the compound sentence on the line.**

1. Laura sings.   We listen.

_____

2. The movie is short.   It is funny.

_____

3. We cheer.   We jump.

_____

4. The day is cold.   The sun is out.

_____

5. We walked to the park.   It was closed.

_____

Name _____ Date _____

Compound Sentences

> A compound sentence is formed when two simple sentences are put together. The simple sentences are combined using a comma and a linking word such as **and** or **but**.
>
> I like apples. Wendy likes pears.
>
> I like apples, **but** Wendy likes pears.

Combine each pair of simple sentences to make a compound sentence. Add a comma and the conjunction *and* or *but*. Write the compound sentence on the line.

1. Mom gets a cart.   Regina pushes.

   _____

2. They buy bread.   They buy cheese.

   _____

3. I am not tired.   Chase is sleepy.

   _____

4. The mango is fresh.   The bread is old.

   _____

Name _____ Date _____

Compound Sentences

> A compound sentence is made up of two simple sentences that are joined by a comma and a conjunction, such as **and**, **but**, **or**, or **so**.
>
> Bo crossed the finish line. The crowd cheered loudly.
>
> Bo crossed the finish line**, and** the crowd cheered loudly.

Combine each pair of simple sentences to make a compound sentence. Add a comma and the conjunction *and* or *but*. Write the compound sentence on the line.

1. Emma went to dinner.   She ate a tasty meal.

   _____

2. The weather was hot.   The cool water tasted good.

   _____

3. The movie was long.   It was interesting.

   _____

4. Ryan ate a pear.   I ate a juicy orange.

   _____

5. I could go for a walk.   I could play inside.

   _____

Name _____ Date _____

Compound Sentences

> A compound sentence is made up of two simple sentences that are joined by a comma and a conjunction, such as **and**, **but**, **or**, or **so**.
>
> It is cool now. It will be warm later.
>
> It is cool now**,** **but** it will be warm later.

Combine each pair of simple sentences to make a compound sentence. Add a comma and a conjunction. Write the compound sentence on the line.

1. It snowed today.   The sky is foggy tonight.

_____

2. We picked many apples.   Pears aren't in season.

_____

3. We can stay up late.   We can go to sleep.

_____

4. You can wear a sweater.   You can put on a coat.

_____

5. Daisy might stay up.   She might read.

_____

Name _____ Date _____

Compound Sentences

> A compound sentence is made up of two simple sentences that are joined by a comma and a conjunction, such as **and**, **but**, **or**, or **so**.
>
> I went to the library. I found a good book.
>
> I went to the library**,** **and** I found a good book.

Combine each pair of simple sentences to make a compound sentence. Add a comma and a conjunction. Write the compound sentence on the line.

1. We went to the water park.   We had fun.

   _____

2. I went down the slide.   Dad swam.

   _____

3. Mom likes tigers.   I like lions.

   _____

4. We can see snakes.   We can see zebras.

   _____

5. I am hungry.   I will make a sandwich.

   _____

Name _____   Date _____

Combine Sentences

> Two related short sentences can be combined into one sentence in order to eliminate repetition. Use a conjunction such as **and**, **but**, **or**, or **so** to join the two sentences.
>
> Henry forgot his homework. Henry forgot his lunch.
>
> Henry forgot his homework **and** his lunch.

Combine each pair of sentences into one sentence.

1. My sister plays the violin. My brother plays the violin.

_____

2. The cat was hungry. The cat was thirsty.

_____

3. Jorge wore blue jeans. Jorge wore a red sweater.

_____

4. Addison has a new notebook. Addison has a new pencil.

_____

5. Zoe opened the door. Zoe opened the window.

_____

Name _____ Date _____

Dictionaries

Use a dictionary to check the spelling, pronunciation, part of speech, and meaning of a word. Words in a dictionary are listed in alphabetical order, from **a** to **z**. When two words begin with the same letter, they are alphabetized by the second letter.

ball (BAUL) *noun* a round object that can be thrown, hit, or kicked

blink (BLINK) *verb* to close and open your eyes fast

Read each group of words. Circle the word that would come first in a dictionary.

1. light   loss   late

2. envy   empty   ever

3. flag   free   foot

Write the words in alphabetical order.

4. trash   tires   tummy   _____

5. poor   plastic   peace   _____

6. share   snack   skip   _____

7. gym   gem   glow   _____

Name _____   Date _____

Dictionaries

Print dictionaries have two guide words on every page. The first guide word represents the first word on the page. The second guide word represents the last word on the page.

large • last

lark (LARK) *noun* 1. a small brown bird
2. a harmless prank
lasso (LA-soh) *noun* a rope with a large loop at the end

For each set of guide words, circle the word that would be on the dictionary page.

1. hungry • hut   horses   hurt   help

2. anger • annoy   animal   America   asleep

3. village • viper   vest   violin   voice

4. class • coat   curl   crash   club

5. kick • knife   knee   koala   key

6. divide • dollar   dye   doctor   damp

7. man • meal   mouse   mild   maze

Name _____ Date _____

Dictionaries

Use a dictionary to check the spelling, pronunciation, part of speech, and meaning of a word. Words in a dictionary are listed in alphabetical order. When two words begin with the same letter, they are alphabetized to the second letter. Print dictionaries have two guide words on every page. The first guide word is the first word on the page, the second is the last word on the page.

pester • pheasant
pester (PES-ter) *verb* to annoy someone
pet (PET) *noun* a tame animal; *verb* to stroke
pheasant (FEH-zunt) *noun* a large bird with a long tail

Write the words in alphabetical order. Remember to alphabetize to the second letter.

1. rain   road   rest _____

2. melon   man   moose _____

3. scrape   stink   shade _____

For each set of guide words, circle the word that would be on the dictionary page.

4. box • branch   blue   brain   butterfly

5. line • load   lizard   lunch   leave

6. angry • apple   arrow   actor   apart

Name _____ Date _____

Formal and Informal Language

Formal language consists of complete sentences and standard grammar. Use formal language in an essay or a letter to the editor. Informal language consists of incomplete sentences and slang. Use informal language in friendly pieces of writing, such as an e-mail or a letter to a friend.

Formal
Good night, Miss Lopez.
In my opinion, this is correct.

Informal
Bye Ashley. I'm out!
I think it's OK, you know?

Circle whether the language in each example is formal or informal.

1. Good morning, Mr. Mayor. May we ask you about the election?

    Formal   Informal

2. Hey! Did you see the cool rainbow? It was awesome!

    Formal   Informal

3. Weather experts are expecting clear weather.

    Formal   Informal

4. Our plans are totally amazing. I'm super excited!

    Formal   Informal

Answer Key

Page 8

Singular and Plural Nouns

Singular nouns tell about one person, place, or thing. Plural nouns tell about more than one person, place, or thing. Add **s** to the end of most nouns to make them plural. For nouns ending in **x**, **z**, **s**, **sh**, or **ch**, add **es**. For nouns ending in a consonant and **y**, change the **y** to **i** and add **es**.

one bat — two **bats**
one box — three **boxes**
one guppy — two **guppies**

Choose the correct noun. Write it on the line.

1. I want two (pony, ponies). _ponies_
2. Mom has one (car, cars). _car_
3. We bought three (dress, dresses). _dresses_
4. We have two (bird, birds) as pets. _birds_
5. I use my (brush, brushes) to paint. _brushes_
6. The (fox, foxes) is orange and white. _fox_
7. I want a (puppy, puppies). _puppy_
8. Look at the family of (bunny, bunnies). _bunnies_

Page 9

Irregular Plural Nouns

A plural noun names more than one person, place, or thing. Regular plural nouns end in **s**. Irregular plural nouns do not have any spelling rules or patterns. Some examples of nouns and their irregular plural forms include: **person/people, mouse/mice, child/children, cactus/cacti, goose/geese, shelf/shelves.**

Choose a noun from the box to complete each sentence. Write it on the line.

| geese | shelf | children | cactus |
| cacti | child | goose | shelves |

1. There are thirty happy _children_ on the playground.
2. The _shelves_ are filled with art supplies.
3. We read a book about a flock of _geese_.
4. We have two _cacti_ growing in the classroom.

Rewrite each sentence with an irregular plural noun.

5. The four white mouse run across the floor.
   The four white mice run across the floor.
6. Many person ate the cake at my party.
   Many people ate the birthday cake.

Page 10

Irregular Plural Nouns

A plural noun names more than one person, place, or thing. Regular plural nouns end in **s**. Irregular plural nouns do not have any spelling rules or patterns. Some examples of nouns and their irregular plural forms include: **foot/feet, calf/calves, wolf/wolves, tooth/teeth, life/lives, woman/women.**

Choose a noun from the box to complete each sentence. Write it on the line.

| life | teeth | wolf | calf |
| tooth | calves | lives | wolves |

1. The _calves_ were born in spring.
2. Dogs bark, but _wolves_ howl.
3. The _teeth_ of a tiger are sharp.
4. Cats do not really have nine _lives_.

Rewrite each sentence with an irregular plural noun.

5. Seven woman work on the farm.
   Seven women work on the farm.
6. There are two goose in the lake.
   There are two geese in the lake.

Page 11

Proper Nouns

Proper nouns name specific people, places, or things. Each main word of a proper noun should begin with a capital letter.

People	Places	Things
Roger	Australia	Pacific Ocean
Taylor	Wyoming	United States
Fred	Delaware	National Zoo

Underline the proper noun in each sentence.

1. I moved from <u>Columbus</u>.
2. My best friend is <u>Rose</u>.
3. He took a trip to <u>Mount Rushmore</u>.

Choose a proper noun from the box to complete each sentence. Write it on the line.

| Washington, D.C. | Lincoln Memorial | Amelia |

4. I visited my friend _Amelia_.
5. She lives in _Washington, D.C._
6. We went to the _Lincoln Memorial_.

Answer Key

Page 12

Proper Nouns

Proper nouns name specific people, places, or things. Each main word of a proper noun should begin with a capital letter.

People	Places	Things
Rahul	California	Statue of Liberty
Thomas	New York	Central Park
Mia	Washington, D.C.	White House

Underline the proper noun in each sentence. Then write the proper noun correctly on the line.

1. I visited the city of <u>austin</u>. _Austin_
2. We made pie with <u>aunt kate</u>. _Aunt Kate_
3. We live on <u>brodie lane</u>. _Brodie Lane_
4. He walks along <u>walnut road</u>. _Walnut Road_

Read each sentence. Then rewrite it correctly on the line.

5. The american museum of natural history is amazing!
   The American Museum of Natural History is amazing!
6. I can't wait to visit utah again!
   I can't wait to visit Utah again!

Page 13

Proper Nouns

Proper nouns name specific people, places, and things. Each main word of a proper noun should begin with a capital letter.

People	Places	Things
Emily	Kansas City	Brooklyn Bridge
Ed Hall	New Mexico	Memorial Day
Mrs. Chopra	Canada	Washington Monument

Underline the proper noun in each sentence. Then write the proper noun correctly on the line.

1. My family went on a trip to <u>nevada</u>. _Nevada_
2. We saw <u>hoover dam</u> the next day. _Hoover Dam_
3. We hiked down the <u>grand canyon</u>. _Grand Canyon_
4. Our guide was named <u>dan smith</u>. _Dan Smith_

Read each sentence. Then rewrite it correctly on the line.

5. The festival is on main street.
   The festival is on Main Street.
6. We will visit mrs. adams next week.
   We will visit Mrs. Adams next week.

Page 14

Collective Nouns

A collective noun names a group of people, places, or things. A collective noun is singular even though it names more than one.

A group of . . .	is called a . . .
students	class
mountains	range
birds	flock

Underline the collective noun in each sentence.

1. I see a <u>bunch</u> of flowers.
2. Is that a <u>bundle</u> of hay?
3. The <u>flock</u> of birds fly together.

Replace each noun in the parentheses ( ) with a collective noun from the box. Write it on the line.

crew	choir	class

4. The (sailor) cleaned the ship. _crew_
5. The (singer) sang a song. _choir_
6. The (student) passed the exam. _class_

Page 15

Possessive Nouns

A possessive shows ownership. Add an apostrophe and **s** to the end of a singular noun to form a possessive. For a plural noun that ends in **s**, add an apostrophe after the **s** to form a possessive.

Singular Possessive	Plural Possessive
Mom's ring	**girls'** shirts
store's parking lot	**customers'** carts
pond's water	**lakes'** shores

Circle the correct possessive. Write it on the line.

1. The _school's_ front door is red. (school's) schools'
2. The _teachers'_ faces are friendly. teacher's (teachers')
3. Our _classroom's_ pet is a guinea pig. (classroom's) classrooms'
4. The _students'_ desks are new. student's (students')

Rewrite each sentence. Replace the underlined words with a possessive.

5. I like <u>the cat that belongs to Lila</u>.
   I like Lila's cat.
6. <u>The shoes of the boys</u> are clean.
   The boys' shoes are clean.

Answer Key

Page 16

Possessive Nouns

1. The yard of my friend is big.
   My friend's yard is big.
2. The leaves of the plant are green.
   The plant's leaves are green.
3. The thorns on the roses are sharp.
   The roses' thorns are sharp.
4. The dog that belongs to Dave plays in the park.
   Dave's dog plays in the park.
5. The toy of the dog is stuck in the bush.
   The dog's toy is stuck in the bush.
6. I sit under the branches of the tree.
   I sit under the tree's branches.

Page 17

Possessive Nouns

1. The gates of the aquarium are open.
   The aquarium's gates are open.
2. I want to see the habitat of the seals.
   I want to see the seals' habitat.
3. The fin of the blue whale is huge!
   The blue whale's fin is huge!
4. Did you see the eggs of the penguin?
   Did you see the penguin's eggs?
5. The tail of the fish is beautiful.
   The fish's tail is beautiful.
6. When is the feeding time of the dolphins?
   When is the dolphins' feeding time?

Page 18

Present Tense Verbs

1. We (visit, visits) the animal shelter. — visit
2. All kinds of animals (live, lives) there. — live
3. A volunteer (take, takes) us on a tour. — takes
4. Black and white cats (run, runs) in circles. — run
5. Puppies (chase, chases) tennis balls. — chase
6. An older brown dog (lick, licks) my hand. — licks
7. Everyone (play, plays) with the puppies. — plays
8. My family (adopt, adopts) the brown dog. — adopts

Page 19

Present Tense Verbs

1. We (see) bats outside at night. — see
2. My dad (know) a lot about bats. — knows
3. He (tell) me all about these flying mammals. — tells
4. Bats (see) in the dark. — see
5. The vampire bat (bite) with its tiny sharp teeth. — bites
6. It (eat) blood! — eats
7. Vampire bats (live) in caves. — live
8. My dad (say) they are not so scary. — says

Answer Key

Page 20

Past Tense Verbs

Past tense verbs tell about actions that already happened. Past tense verbs often end in **-ed**. This is true whether the subject is singular or plural.
  Maisie **jumped** rope.
  We all **jumped** rope.

Write the past tense form of the verb in the parentheses ( ).

1. Last winter, Mom (order) seeds for her vegetable garden.
   ordered
2. Together, we (plant) the seeds in the spring.
   planted
3. I (water) the seeds every day. watered
4. I (watch) the seeds become vegetable plants.
   watched
5. The sun (warm) them. warmed
6. We (pick) and ate vegetables all summer.
   picked

Page 21

Irregular Past Tense Verbs

Past tense verbs tell about actions that already happened. Past tense verbs that do not end in **-ed** are irregular. Some examples of verbs and their irregular past tense forms include **fall/fell**, **slide/slid**, **tell/told**, **take/took**.

Choose a past tense verb from the box to complete each sentence. Write it on the line.

| take | told | slide | fell |
| fall | tell | took | slid |

1. I fell last week in the rain.
2. We took a walk in the park.
3. I slid across the wet sidewalk.
4. I told my sister about it.

Rewrite each sentence with the past tense form of the underlined verb.

5. Many snowflakes fall.
   Many snowflakes fell.
6. We slide down the hill.
   We slid down the hill.

Page 22

Irregular Past Tense Verbs

Past tense verbs tell about actions that already happened. Past tense verbs that do not end in **-ed** are irregular. Some examples of verbs and their irregular past tense forms include **begin/began**, **hide/hid**, **throw/threw**, **dig/dug**, **grow/grew**, **see/saw**.

Choose a past tense verb from the box to complete each sentence. Write it on the line.

| hid | throw | grew | dig |
| grow | hide | dug | threw |

1. My kitten grew big this year.
2. Today, I threw a ball of yarn to him.
3. He hid the yarn behind the couch.
4. He dug it out a few hours later.

Rewrite each sentence with the past tense form of the underlined verb.

5. The exam begin at 9:00 a.m.
   The exam began at 9:00 a.m.
6. They see the movie.
   They saw the movie.

Page 23

Irregular Past Tense Verbs

Past tense verbs tell about actions that already happened. Past tense verbs that do not end in **-ed** are irregular. Some examples of verbs and their irregular past tense forms include **get/got**, **do/did**, **ride/rode**, **buy/bought**, **ring/rang**.

Choose a past tense verb from the box to complete each sentence. Write it on the line.

| rode | do | ring | got |
| get | rang | did | ride |

1. The bell rang at the end of class.
2. Sally rode her bike around the block.
3. I did well on the spelling quiz.
4. Mom got a new shirt from the store.

Rewrite each sentence with the past tense form of the underlined verb.

5. They ride in the car.
   They rode in the car.
6. They buy groceries.
   They bought groceries.

Answer Key

Page 24

Irregular Past Tense Verbs

Past tense verbs tell about actions that already happened. Past tense verbs that do not end in **-ed** are irregular. Some examples of verbs and their irregular past tense forms include **send/sent, say/said, leave/left, wear/wore, grow/grew, see/saw**.

Choose the correct verb. Write it on the line.

1. I (leave, left) my jacket at home. _left_
2. Mom (said, say) the weather was cold. _said_
3. I wish I (wore, wear) my jacket. _wore_
4. Mom (send, sent) my jacket to school. _sent_

Rewrite each sentence using the past tense form of the underlined verb.

5. I send a letter.
   I sent a letter.
6. I say good morning.
   I said good morning.

Page 25

Future Tense Verbs

Future tense verbs tell about actions that will happen at a later time. To form the future tense, place the word **will** in front of the verb.
  Gillian **will watch** her baby sister.
  Mom **will bake** a cake.

Write the future tense form of the verb in the parentheses ( ).

1. Tara (win) the race. _will win_
2. She (practice) every day. _will practice_
3. Dad (help) Tara stay focused. _will help_
4. He (be) her coach. _will be_
5. Tara (eat) healthfully to stay in shape. _will eat_
6. She (buy) new sneakers. _will buy_
7. Dad (pay) for them. _will pay_
8. Tara (sleep) eight hours a night. _will sleep_

Page 26

Future Tense Verbs

Future tense verbs tell about actions that will happen at a later time. To form the future tense, place the word **will** in front of the verb.
  Hannah **will run** in the race.
  We **will cheer** for her.

Write the future tense form of the verb in the parentheses ( ).

1. Neil (play) hockey this winter. _will play_
2. He (need) lots of equipment. _will need_
3. Dad (take) him shopping. _will take_
4. They (shop) at the secondhand store. _will shop_

Rewrite each sentence with the future tense form of the underlined verb.

5. The equipment cost much less there.
   The equipment will cost much less there.
6. They save money and the environment.
   They will save money and the environment.

Page 27

Verb Tenses

The tense of a verb tells when the action happens. To form the past tense of most verbs, add **ed**. For the present tense, use the verb alone or add an **s** or **-es**. To form the future tense, add the word **will** in front of the verb.

Past
Last year I **learned** to swim.

Present
Now, I **learn** to play baseball.

Future
Next year, I **will learn** to play tennis.

Read each sentence. Write *past*, *present*, or *future* for the underlined verb.

1. We keep a monarch butterfly in our classroom. _present_
2. The butterfly started as an egg. _past_
3. Then the egg hatched into a caterpillar. _past_
4. We watched the caterpillar turn into a butterfly. _past_
5. The black-and-orange butterfly lives in a cage. _present_

Choose the correct verb. Write it on the line.

6. Tomorrow we (set, will set) the butterfly free. _will set_
7. It (flew, will fly) south for the winter. _will fly_

Answer Key

Page 28

Verb Tenses

The tense of a verb tells when the action happens. To form the past tense of most verbs, add **ed**. For the present tense, use the verb alone or add an **s** or **-es**. To form the future tense, add the word **will** in front of the verb.

Past	Present	Future
This morning, Mom **walked** the dog.	Now Dad and I **walk** him.	Tonight, Dad **will walk** him.

Choose the correct verb. Write it on the line.

1. Yesterday, I (lost, will lose) my baseball glove. _lost_
2. I (think, will think) I left it at the field. _think_
3. After school today, Mom and I (looked, will look) for it. _will look_
4. I (hope, hoped) it is there. _hope_
5. It (was, will be) a birthday present. _was_

Read each sentence. Write past, present, or future for the underlined verb.

6. We searched in the dugout. _past_
7. I found the glove under the bench. _past_

Page 29

Collective Nouns with Matching Verbs

A collective noun names a group of people, places, or things. A collective noun is singular even though it names more than one. Use singular verbs with collective nouns. A singular verb ends in **s**.

Our **family** eats together.
The **jury** listens to the judge.

Underline the collective noun in each sentence. Then rewrite the sentence with the correct form of the verb.

1. Our troop camp in the forest.
   Our troop camps in the forest.
2. The forest come alive.
   The forest comes alive.
3. A flock of birds sing in the tree.
   A flock of birds sings in the tree.
4. A herd of deer run in the meadow.
   A herd of deer runs in the meadow.
5. A school of fish swim in the lake.
   A school of fish swims in the lake.

Page 30

Singular and Plural Nouns with Matching Verbs

In a sentence, the noun, or subject, and the verb must match. A singular noun takes a singular verb. A plural noun takes a plural verb.

The **rabbit** hops.
The three **rabbits** hop.

Choose the correct verb. Write it on the line.

1. The spider _spins_ a web. (spin, spins)
2. The ants _crawl_ on the log. (crawl, crawls)
3. The bees _buzz_ in the field. (buzz, buzzes)
4. The butterfly _spreads_ its wings. (spread, spreads)
5. The worms _slide_ through the dirt. (slide, slides)

Read each sentence. Choose the correct verb in the parentheses ( ). Write it on the line.

6. Frogs (jump, jumps) high. _jump_
7. The bird (sing, sings) a song. _sings_

Page 31

Personal Pronouns

Pronouns are words that take the place of nouns. **I, me, you, he, him, she, her, it, we, us, you, they,** and **them** are personal pronouns. They are used to refer to a specific person or thing, and to avoid repetition of the noun.

Noun	Personal Pronoun
Julio got his own key.	**He** got his own key.
Julio put the **key** on a key chain.	Julio put **it** on a key chain.

Choose a personal pronoun from the box to complete each sentence. Write it on the line.

he	him	it	they	them

1. Mom bought a violin for _him_.
2. _He_ put the violin in a safe place.
3. His friends Billy and Eric asked to see _it_.
4. _They_ were so excited!
5. Julio asked _them_ to be careful.
6. Julio did not want to break _it_.

Answer Key

Page 32

Personal Pronouns

Pronouns are words that take the place of nouns. **I, me, you, he, him, she, her, it, we, us, you, they,** and **them** are personal pronouns. They are used to refer to a specific person or thing, and to avoid repetition of the noun.

Noun	Personal Pronoun
Kara buys a bike.	**She** buys a bike.
Kara rides the bike before **Kara** buys it.	**Kara** rides the bike before **she** buys it.

Write the personal pronoun *he, she, him, her, it, they,* or *them* for the underlined word or words.

1. <u>Kara and Dad</u> went for a bike ride. _they_
2. <u>Kara</u> got a flat tire. _she_
3. The flat made <u>Kara and Dad</u> stop. _them_
4. <u>Dad</u> had a pump and a patch. _he_
5. Dad helped <u>Kara</u> fix the flat tire. _her_
6. <u>The tire</u> was good as new. _it_
7. Kara thanked <u>Dad</u> and they kept riding. _him_
8. <u>Kara and Dad</u> finished the bike trail. _they_

Page 33

Possessive Pronouns

Pronouns take the place of nouns. Possessive pronouns tell who or what owns something. **My, mine, our, ours, its, his, her, hers, their, theirs, your,** and **yours** are possessive pronouns.
The bird built a nest in **Fiona's** tree.
The bird built a nest in **her** tree.
The bird cleaned **the bird's** feathers.
The bird cleaned **its** feathers.

Read each sentence. Underline the possessive pronoun.

1. The bird used twigs to build <u>its</u> nest.
2. I can see the nest from <u>our</u> bathroom window.
3. <u>My</u> whole family watches the bird's nest.
4. We use <u>our</u> binoculars to see better.

Write the correct possessive pronoun for the underlined word or words.

5. Fiona thinks the nest is <u>Fiona's</u>. _hers_
6. That is because it is in <u>Fiona's</u> tree. _her_
7. I bet the bird thinks it is <u>the bird's</u> nest. _its_

Page 34

Possessive Pronouns

Pronouns take the place of nouns. Possessive pronouns tell who or what owns something. **My, mine, our, ours, its, his, her, hers, their, theirs, your,** and **yours** are possessive pronouns.
We call **Mom's** parents Nana and Poppy.
We call **her** parents Nana and Poppy.
We call **Dad's** parents Grandma and Grandpa.
We call **his** parents Grandma and Grandpa.

Choose a personal pronoun from the box to complete each sentence. Write it on the line.

| her | their | our | his | theirs | my |

1. I packed _my_ suitcase last night.
2. My brothers packed _theirs_ also.
3. We are going to visit _our_ grandparents.
4. Mom will be happy to see _her_ parents.
5. Dad calls them _his_ second parents.
6. We will stay at _their_ house for a week.

Page 35

Indefinite Pronouns

Pronouns are words that take the place of nouns. Indefinite pronouns don't refer to a specific person or thing.
There was **nothing** left to eat.
Everybody went home.

Read each sentence. Underline the indefinite pronoun.

1. <u>Somebody</u> spilled a glass of milk.
2. <u>Everybody's</u> milk spilled.
3. <u>Nobody</u> knew who did it.
4. <u>Everybody</u> pointed at the cat.
5. The cat could not say <u>anything</u>.

Choose the correct indefinite pronoun. Write it on the line.

6. (Nobody, Nothing) wanted to clean the mess.
   nobody
7. Mom said (anything, everyone) should help clean up.
   everyone

Answer Key

Page 36

Indefinite Pronouns

Pronouns are words that take the place of nouns. Indefinite pronouns don't refer to a specific person or thing.
  Did **anyone** lose money?
  Someone found two dollars in the cafeteria.

Choose an indefinite pronoun from the box to complete each sentence. Write it on the line.

| anybody | anything | everyone | somewhere | nobody |

1. This road must lead _somewhere_.
2. Do you have _anything_ to say?
3. We need a bus that will fit _everyone_.
4. The phone kept ringing because _nobody_ was home.
5. _Nobody_ can find my baseball glove.
6. Does _anybody_ have a pencil I can borrow?
7. The stadium was empty because there was _nobody_ at the game.

Page 37

Reflexive Pronouns

Pronouns are words that take the place of nouns. Reflexive pronouns refer back to the subject and always end in **-self** or **-selves**. **Myself, yourself, himself, herself, itself, ourselves, yourselves,** and **themselves** are reflexive pronouns.
  The cat saved **the cat** from the fire.
  The cat saved **itself** from the fire.
  My cousins take care of **my cousins**.
  My cousins take care of **themselves**.

Read each sentence. Underline the reflexive pronoun.

1. She hurt _herself_ when she fell.
2. We blame _ourselves_ for the low attendance of the event.
3. My little brother can feed _himself_.
4. You can help _yourself_ to more food.

Read each sentence. Write *themselves*, *himself*, or *herself* for the underlined word or words.

5. Lisa wrote _Lisa_ a note. _herself_
6. The students lined _the students_ up for lunch. _themselves_
7. My grandfather taught _my grandfather_ to read. _himself_

Page 38

Reflexive Pronouns

Pronouns are words that take the place of nouns. Reflexive pronouns refer back to the subject and always end in **-self** or **-selves**. **Myself, yourself, himself, herself, itself, ourselves, yourselves,** and **themselves** are reflexive pronouns.
  Ricky bought **Ricky** a new camera.
  Ricky bought **himself** a new camera.
  The teammates took a picture of the **teammates**.
  The teammates took a picture of **themselves**.

From the box, choose the possessive pronoun that best completes each sentence. Write it on the line.

| herself | myself | itself | ourselves | himself | themselves |

1. I saw _myself_ in the mirror.
2. My baby brother sings to _himself_.
3. Our cat spends hours grooming _itself_.
4. The students were proud of _themselves_.
5. Mom poured _herself_ a cup of coffee.
6. We read to _ourselves_ during independent time.

Page 39

Adjectives

Adjectives are words that describe nouns, adjectives, or adverbs. Adjectives give details about people, places, and things. They tell about size, color, number, and kind. In the phrase *the blue rug*, the adjective **blue** tells the color of the noun **rug**.

Read each sentence. Circle the adjective and underline the noun it describes.

1. Jasmine refused to clean her (messy) room.
2. She was looking for her (orange) backpack.
3. Anya enjoys cooking (delicious) food.
4. He dislikes washing (dirty) dishes.
5. Bryn thinks that the park is (small).
6. That (annoying) alarm clock keeps buzzing!
7. Luis's (youngest) brother misbehaves.
8. Dan's (older) cousin is nice.
9. The town has a lot of (pretty) houses.
10. The theater has a (big) stage.

Answer Key

Page 40

Adjectives

Adjectives are words that describe nouns, adjectives, or adverbs. Adjectives give details about people, places, and things. They tell about size, color, number, and kind. In the phrase *the brown dog*, the adjective **brown** tells the color of the noun **dog**.

Read each sentence. Underline the adjective and circle the noun it describes.

1. Nicole wore <u>red</u> (shoes) to the party.
2. Max bakes <u>delicious</u> (cakes).
3. We were excited to see our <u>old</u> (friends).
4. Elena planted <u>purple</u> (flowers).
5. Mike draws <u>beautiful</u> (pictures).
6. Andrew collects <u>old</u> (stamps).
7. My cat doesn't like <u>loud</u> (noises).
8. Liam played <u>beautiful</u> (music).

Page 41

Adjectives

Adjectives are words that describe nouns, adjectives, or adverbs. Adjectives give details about people, places, and things. They tell about size, color, number, and kind. In the sentence *Olga gave me two flowers*, the adjective **two** tells the number of the noun **flowers**.

Read each sentence. Underline the adjective and circle the noun it describes.

1. I am a <u>talented</u> (artist).
2. I like to paint <u>big</u> (pictures).
3. I want to paint this <u>sunny</u> (park).
4. I like to draw with my <u>red</u> (marker).
5. Will you take <u>one</u> (picture) with me?
6. I need a <u>white</u> (dress).
7. I love <u>rainy</u> (weather).
8. Luca bought <u>green</u> (apples).

Page 42

Adjectives

Adjectives are words that describe nouns, adjectives, or adverbs. Adjectives give details about people, places, and things. They tell about size, color, number, and kind. In the phrase *the slippery stones*, the adjective **slippery** tells the kind of **stones**.

Read each sentence. Underline the adjective and circle the noun it describes.

1. Carlos has <u>two</u> (sisters).
2. Everyone enjoyed the <u>delicious</u> (meal).
3. We woke up to a <u>cloudy</u> (sky).
4. A <u>giant</u> (tree) blocked the trail.

Choose an adjective from the box to complete each sentence. Write it on the line.

| green | deep | small | two |

5. The __small__ kitten started to purr.
6. Eliza checks out __two__ library books.
7. Ted wore a __green__ sweater.
8. After the storm, we splashed in the __deep__ puddles.

Page 43

Adverbs

Adverbs describe verbs, nouns, adjectives, and adverbs. They give details about how, when, or where an action happens. Other examples of adverbs include **before**, **here**, **later**, and **there**.

We sing **loudly**.   We sang this song **before**.
We stand **here**.   Our teacher stands **nearby**.

Read each sentence. Circle the verb and underline the adverb.

1. We (visited) the lake <u>yesterday</u>.
2. The children (played) <u>quietly</u>.
3. The turtles (moved) <u>slowly</u>.
4. We (fed) bread to the ducks <u>later</u>.
5. Dad (swam) <u>nearby</u>.

Underline the adverb in each sentence. Then circle whether the adverb tells how, when, or where.

6. I <u>always</u> brush my teeth.
    How   (When)   Where
7. Let's eat <u>there</u>!
    How   When   (Where)

Answer Key

Page 44

Adverbs

Adverbs describe verbs, nouns, adjectives, and adverbs. They give details about how, when, or where an action happens.
- We spoke **clearly**.
- We recited the poem **before**.
- I left my book **somewhere**.
- James **eagerly** stood up.

Read each sentence. Circle the verb and underline the adverb.

1. I happily (volunteered) to help shovel the snow.
2. The workers (drove) to the office daily.
3. We (held) the presentation outdoors.
4. We all (performed) beautifully.
5. We (threw) a party afterward.

Underline the adverb in each sentence. Then circle whether the adverb tells who, when, or where.

6. Weeds grow everywhere.   How   When   (Where)
7. Amanda carefully pulls them.   (How)   When   Where
8. Tomato plants will sprout soon.   How   (When)   Where

Page 45

Adjectives and Adverbs

Adjectives describe nouns, adjectives, and adverbs. Adverbs describe verbs, nouns, adjectives, and adverbs.
- **Adjective:** My new shoes are **perfect**!
- **Adverb:** My new shoes fit **perfectly**!

Choose the adjective or the adverb. Write it on the line.

1. The __short__ flight took only an hour.
   (shortly   short)
2. Juan __excitedly__ waited for the show to start.
   (excitedly   exciting)
3. I rode my scooter __quickly__.
   (quickly   quick)
4. Jen __happily__ helped Max with his homework.
   (happily   happy)
5. We went to the theater to hear __beautiful__ music.
   (beautifully   beautiful)

Page 46

Adjectives and Adverbs

Adjectives describe nouns, adjectives, and adverbs. Adverbs describe verbs, nouns, adjectives, and adverbs.
- **Adjective:** The **brave** firefighters put out the fire.
- **Adverb:** The firefighters **bravely** put out the fire.

Choose the correct adjective or adverb from the box to complete each sentence. Write it on the line.

| strange | strangely | happy | loudly |
| happily | loud | sweet | sweetly |

1. Nick picked up the __strange__ object to take a closer look.
2. This cake is __sweet__.
3. I sang __loudly__ to the music.
4. I ran __happily__ toward the park.
5. My winter jacket fit __strangely__ after I grew.
6. The marching band was so __loud__!
7. My sister was __happy__ to knit me a new sweater.

Page 47

Comparatives and Superlatives

Use comparative adjectives and adverbs to compare two people, places, or things. Add **-er** to most one-syllable adjectives and adverbs to compare two. Add **-est** to form the superlative to compare more than two.

Adjectives
My turtle is **smaller** than my gerbil.
My fish is the **smallest** of all.

Adverbs
Buddy runs **faster** than Rusty.
The black dog runs the **fastest** of all.

Underline the comparative or superlative adjective or adverb in each sentence. Then circle whether it compares two or more than two.

1. Jen arrived sooner than Scott.   (two)   more than two
2. Angelo studied harder than I did.   (two)   more than two
3. She is the smartest person I know.   two   (more than two)

Choose the comparative adjective or the comparative adverb. Write it on the line.

4. The weather is __colder__ today than yesterday.
   (colder, coldest)
5. My kite flew __higher__ than Evan's kite.   (higher, highest)

Answer Key

Page 48

Comparatives and Superlatives

Comparatives compare two or more people, places, or things. Superlatives compare three or more. For an adjective or adverb that has more than one syllable and does not end in **y**, place the word **more** or **most** in front of the word to make the comparative. **More** compares two things and **most** compares more than two things.

Adjectives	Adverbs
Our porch is **more** peaceful than the living room.	Ava rides **more** carefully than Oliver.
My room is the **most** peaceful place of all.	Frankie rides **most** carefully of all.

Underline the comparative or superlative in each sentence. Then circle whether it compares two or more than two.

1. My sister dances <u>more gracefully</u> than I do.
   (two)   more than two

2. Carly is the <u>most talented</u> singer in the choir.
   two   (more than two)

3. Mr. Bruno is the <u>most skillful</u> art teacher.
   two   (more than two)

4. Of all our neighbors, our family hosts parties <u>most often</u>.
   two   (more than two)

Page 49

Comparatives and Superlatives

Add **-er** to most one-syllable adjectives and adverbs to compare two (comparative). Add **-est** to most one-syllable adjectives and adverbs to compare more than two (superlative). If an adjective or adverb has more than one syllable and does not end in **y**, use **more** to compare two things and **most** to compare more than two things.

Compare Two	Compare More than Two
We took the **shorter** of the two trails.	The east trail is the **longest** of all.
I walked **slower** than Liam.	Karen walked the **fastest**.
This trail is **more rugged** than the last.	Which trail is the **most scenic**?

Underline the comparative or superlative adjective or adverb. Circle whether it compares two or more than two.

1. Carlos worked <u>harder</u> than I did.
   (two)   more than two

2. His pastries were <u>better</u> than mine.
   (two)   more than two

3. The <u>most talented</u> chef won the contest.
   two   (more than two)

4. Snowboarding seems <u>more difficult</u> than skiing.
   (two)   more than two

Page 50

Prepositions

Prepositions connect two or more words in a sentence and show how they are related. Some prepositions show where something is. Others show where or when something happens.
This book belongs **in** the library.
The next game is **on** Saturday.

Circle the preposition in each sentence.

1. Aldo poured milk (on) his cereal.
2. We went (to) the movies.
3. The visitor left (after) lunch.
4. The vines grew (up) the wall.
5. Nadia looked (at) the painting.
6. The dog climbed (over) the fence.
7. I cheered (during) the game.
8. My house is (by) the school.

Page 51

Conjunctions

Use conjunctions such as **and**, **or**, **but**, **so**, or **because** to combine shorter sentences.
I play soccer. I play baseball.
I play soccer **and** baseball.

Combine each pair of sentences using the conjunction in the parentheses ( ). Write the new sentence on the line.

1. I ate an apple. I ate a pear. (and)
   I ate an apple and a pear.

2. We may go today. We may go tomorrow. (or)
   We may go today or tomorrow.

3. Would you like milk? Would you like juice? (or)
   Would you like milk or juice?

4. Yesterday was cold. It was sunny. (but)
   Yesterday was cold but it was sunny.

5. The game ended. We went home. (so)
   The game ended so we went home.

6. I went to sleep. I was tired. (because)
   I went to sleep because I was tired.

Answer Key

Page 52

Articles

The words **a**, **an**, and **the** are articles. Use **the** to tell about an exact person, place, or thing. Use **a** or **an** to tell about any person, place, or thing. Use **a** before a consonant sound and **an** before a vowel sound.
- Dad went to **the** store.
- He wanted to buy **an** umbrella.
- It was **a** rainy day.

Choose the correct article. Write it on the line.

1. Lena went to (a, the) kitchen. _the_
2. She opened (an, the) refrigerator. _the_
3. She grabbed (a, an) apple. _an_
4. She got (a, the) peanut butter. _the_
5. Then she looked for (a, the) plate. _a_
6. She could only find (a, the) bowl. _a_
7. She sat down at (a, the) table. _the_
8. She ate (a, the) sandwich. _the_

Page 53

Demonstratives

This, **that**, **these**, and **those** are demonstratives. Demonstratives tell about specific people, places, or things. Use **this** and **these** to talk about things that are nearby. Use **that** and **those** to talk about things that are far away. Use **this** and **that** with singular nouns, and **these** and **those** with plural nouns.
- **This** is my desk.
- **That** locker is mine.
- **These** markers go in my desk.
- **Those** markers belong to Ricky.

Choose the correct demonstrative. Write it on the line.

1. (This, These) is the block where I live. _This_
2. (This, Those) are my neighbors across the street. _Those_
3. (This, These) is my house. _This_
4. (That, Those) is my mom's car in the driveway. _That_
5. (Those, These) are my house keys. _These_
6. (That, This) is my cat in the upstairs window. _That_

Page 54

Commas in Series

Use commas to separate three or more words in a series.
Ivan grows lettuce, tomatoes, and cucumbers.

Read each sentence. Write commas where needed.

1. We walk, skip, and run in gym class.
2. Marco, Adam, and Shawn play hockey.
3. The puppy has brown, gray, and white fur.
4. We had salad, chicken, and rice for dinner.
5. Dad bought cereal, chips, and fruit at the store.

Rewrite each sentence with the correct punctuation.

6. Mrs. Dooley visited Arizona Nevada and New Mexico.
   Mrs. Dooley visited Arizona, Nevada, and New Mexico.
7. She traveled by car train and plane.
   She traveled by car, train, and plane.
8. Theo James and Yoko play guitar.
   Theo, James, and Yoko play guitar.

Page 55

Commas in Dates and Series

Use commas in dates, and to separate three or more words in a series.
The school opened on Monday, October 6, 1980.
Ariel likes to sing, dance, and act.

Read each sentence. Write commas where needed.

1. My sister plays basketball, soccer, and softball.
2. I found an old newspaper dated Saturday, March 3, 1934.
3. Mom grows pink, purple, and yellow flowers.

Rewrite each sentence with the correct punctuation.

4. The triplets are named Luke Matt and Daniel.
   The triplets are named Luke, Matt, and Daniel.
5. They were born on Tuesday November 16 2010.
   The triplets were born on Tuesday, November 16, 2010.
6. Vivian wore a hat mittens and a scarf.
   Vivian wore a hat, mittens, and a scarf.

Answer Key

Page 56

Commas in Introductory Phrases and Clauses

A comma (,) is used to set off an introductory phrase or clause in a sentence.
Later in the day, we will visit the museum.
Once we were on our way, we were fine.

Read each sentence. Write commas where needed.

1. Before we went shopping, Mom clipped coupons.
2. When the rain started, we ran inside the house.
3. While we were in the park, I saw three squirrels.
4. After jumping in a puddle, Nina had to dry off.
5. To prepare for the picnic, we made some lemonade.

Rewrite each sentence with the correct punctuation.

6. Before Sara left the party she said good-bye to everyone.
   Before Sara left the party, she said good-bye to everyone.
7. While we are watching the movie let's eat our snacks.
   While we are watching the movie, let's eat our snacks.

Page 57

Commas in Greetings

Letters or e-mails begin with a greeting. A greeting consists of a word such as **Dear** or **Hi** and the name of the person to whom you are writing, followed by a comma. Every word in a greeting should begin with a capital letter.
Dear Mrs. Grant,   **Hi** Carlos,   **Dear** Diary,

Read each greeting. Write a comma where needed.

1. Dear Tony,
   Will you come to my party?
2. Dear Diary,
   I rode my scooter to school.
3. Hi Kelsey,
   Meet me at the mall.
4. Dear Evan,
   Did you find your gear?
5. Hi Uncle Mike,
   How are you?
6. Hi Grandma,
   I miss you.

Rewrite the letter opening correctly on the lines.

Dear Andy Thank you for the gift.
Dear Andy,
Thank you for the gift.

Page 58

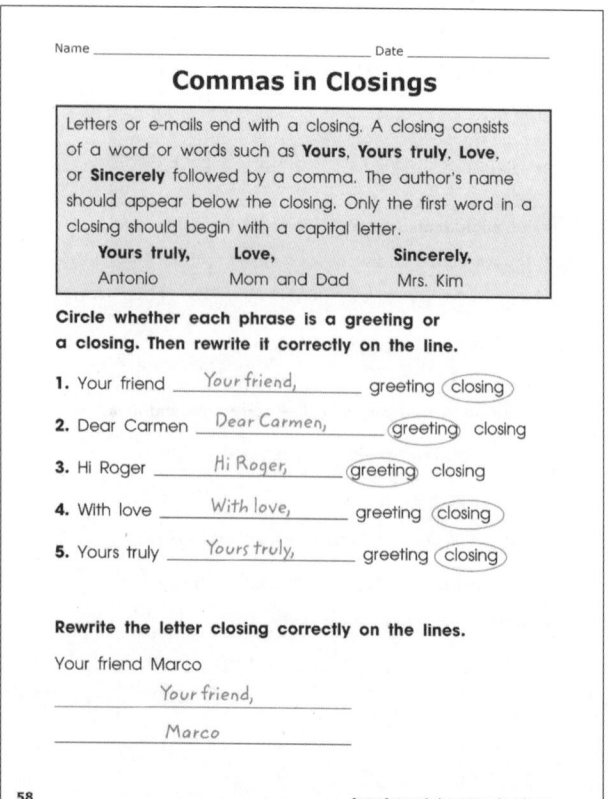

Commas in Closings

Letters or e-mails end with a closing. A closing consists of a word or words such as **Yours**, **Yours truly**, **Love**, or **Sincerely** followed by a comma. The author's name should appear below the closing. Only the first word in a closing should begin with a capital letter.
Yours truly,   **Love,**   **Sincerely,**
Antonio   Mom and Dad   Mrs. Kim

Circle whether each phrase is a greeting or a closing. Then rewrite it correctly on the line.

1. Your friend _Your friend,_ greeting (closing)
2. Dear Carmen _Dear Carmen,_ (greeting) closing
3. Hi Roger _Hi Roger,_ (greeting) closing
4. With love _With love,_ greeting (closing)
5. Yours truly _Yours truly,_ greeting (closing)

Rewrite the letter closing correctly on the lines.

Your friend Marco
Your friend,
Marco

Page 59

Commas in Greetings and Closings

Letters or e-mails begin with a greeting and end with a closing. Greetings and closings are always followed by a comma.
Dear Cole,   **Hi** Kate,
I had fun at your party.   We won the game!
Your pal,   **Yours joyfully,**
Inez   Brian

Rewrite each greeting or closing correctly on the line.

1. hi john
   Hi John,
2. your pal
   Your pal,
3. dear aunt mary
   Dear Aunt Mary,
4. best wishes
   Best wishes,
5. dear sister
   Dear Sister,
6. until then
   Until then,

Form a closing by writing the words in the correct order. Remember to add a comma.

son   your   loving
Your loving son,

Answer Key

Page 60

Commas in Greetings and Closings

Letters or e-mails begin with a greeting and end with a closing. Greetings and closings are always followed by a comma.

Dear Mayor Brown,
Please consider my plan
for the new park.
Sincerely,
Mrs. Palmer

Hi Amir,
I miss you so much!
Love,
Kiki

Circle whether each phrase is a greeting or a closing. Then rewrite it correctly on the line.

1. Hi Tina — Hi Tina, (greeting) closing
2. All my best — All my best, greeting (closing)
3. Dear Diary — Dear Diary, (greeting) closing
4. Your friend — Your friend, greeting (closing)
5. With love — With love, greeting (closing)

Form a greeting by writing the words in the correct order. Remember to add a comma.

Sue   Aunt   Dear

Dear Aunt Sue,

Page 61

End Marks

An end mark is the punctuation that comes at the end of a sentence.
- Statements or telling sentences end in a period: .
- Sentences that ask a question end in question mark: ?
- Sentences that show strong feeling end in an exclamation mark: !
- Sentences that give commands usually end in a period: .

Read each sentence. Write the correct end mark.

1. I love amusement parks **!**
2. We visit one every summer **.**
3. This summer we will go to Lake Compounce **.**
4. Have you ever been there **?**
5. Come with us **.**
6. We are leaving tomorrow **.**

Page 62

End Marks

An end mark is the punctuation that comes at the end of a sentence.
- Statements or telling sentences end in a period: .
- Sentences that ask a question end in question mark: ?
- Sentences that show strong feeling end in an exclamation mark: !
- Sentences that give commands end in a period: . or an exclamation mark: !

Read each sentence. Write the correct end mark.

1. I know lots about sharks **.**
2. The shark has thousands of sharp teeth **!**
3. The shark's eyes look a lot like ours **.**
4. Sharks were here even before the dinosaurs **!**
5. I would love to see a shark one day **!**
6. Do you want to learn about sharks **?**
7. I have some books you can borrow **.**

Page 63

Contractions

A contraction is a shortened form of a word or words. An apostrophe (') replaces the dropped letter or letters in a contraction.

Words	Contraction
will not	won't
I have	I've
could not	couldn't
does not	doesn't

Choose a contraction from the box to take the place of the underlined words in each sentence. Write the contraction on the line.

| I've | couldn't | didn't |
| won't | she'd | wasn't |

1. Robert <u>was not</u> at the show. **wasn't**
2. He <u>could not</u> get a ticket. **couldn't**
3. He <u>did not</u> want to stay home. **didn't**
4. <u>I have</u> asked him to come over. **I've**
5. He <u>will not</u> come alone. **won't**
6. He said <u>she would</u> bring a friend. **she'd**

Conquer Grammar • Grade 2 • © Newmark Learning, LLC

Answer Key

Page 64

Contractions

A contraction is a shortened form of a word or words. An apostrophe replaces the dropped letter or letters in a contraction.
I will go to the party.   **I'll** go to the party.

Underline the contraction in each sentence. Then write the words that make the contraction.

1. <u>Let's</u> meet before the movie starts. _Let us_
2. <u>Doesn't</u> the rain get in the way of the parade? _does not_
3. I guess <u>we'll</u> see Ava when we get there. _we will_
4. I <u>don't</u> like the heat. _do not_
5. It <u>isn't</u> fair that we have to stay inside! _is not_
6. Olivia <u>didn't</u> get my letter, so I will resend it. _did not_
7. Zeke is not able to go to the store today, so <u>he'll</u> go tomorrow. _he will_
8. Mom said <u>they're</u> almost here! _they are_

Page 65

Contractions

A contraction is a shortened form of a word or words. An apostrophe (') replaces the dropped letter or letters in a contraction.

Words	Contraction
do not	don't
cannot	can't
has not	hasn't

Underline the contraction in each sentence. Then write the word or words that make the contraction.

1. <u>I've</u> never been to the carnival. _I have_
2. Maddie <u>hasn't</u> bought the book yet. _has not_
3. Jenna <u>can't</u> find her cat. _cannot_
4. <u>Who'll</u> be coming to the bake sale? _Who will_
5. <u>Don't</u> forget to let the dog out. _Do not_

Rewrite each sentence. Replace the underlined words with a contraction.

6. The catcher <u>did not</u> come to the softball game.
   The catcher didn't come to the softball game.
7. Amanda <u>could not</u> bring her brother to school.
   Amanda couldn't bring her brother to school.

Page 66

Contractions

A contraction is a shortened form of a word or words. An apostrophe (') replaces the dropped letter or letters in a contraction.

Words	Contraction
does not	doesn't
who will	who'll
we have	we've
are not	aren't

Underline the contraction in each sentence. Then write the words that make the contraction.

1. Nick <u>hasn't</u> read the book. _has not_
2. Nadia <u>doesn't</u> have an extra copy. _does not_
3. <u>Who'll</u> lend Nick the book? _Who will_
4. <u>We've</u> seen plenty of copies in the library. _We have_

Rewrite each sentence. Replace the underlined words with a contraction.

5. The books <u>are not</u> on the table.
   The books aren't on the table.
6. Tito <u>is not</u> here yet.
   Tito isn't here yet.

Page 67

Contractions

A contraction is a shortened form of a word or words. An apostrophe (') replaces the dropped letter or letters in a contraction.

Words	Contraction
did not	didn't
who is	who's
I have	I've
I will	I'll
we are	we're

Underline each contraction. On the line, write the two words that form it.

1. The team <u>didn't</u> play very well. _did not_
2. We <u>weren't</u> impressed by their teamwork. _were not_
3. <u>Who's</u> going to the carnival next week? _Who is_
4. <u>I've</u> already bought my tickets. _I have_

Rewrite each sentence. Replace the underlined words with a contraction.

5. <u>I will</u> see you at the theater!
   I'll see you at the theater!
6. <u>We are</u> getting there early.
   We're getting there early.

Answer Key

Page 68

Contractions and Possessive Nouns

A contraction is a shortened form of a word or words. An apostrophe replaces the dropped letter or letters in a contraction. Possessive nouns show that a person, place, or thing has or owns something. Add an apostrophe (') and an **s** to make a singular possessive noun.

Contraction	Possessive
Emma's my best friend.	**Emma's** sweater is red.

For each sentence, circle whether the underlined word is a contraction or a possessive.

1. Is Kyra's birthday next week? Contraction **(Possessive)**
2. Let's throw a surprise party! **(Contraction)** Possessive
3. She'll be happy. **(Contraction)** Possessive
4. Jack has her friends' addresses. Contraction **(Possessive)**

Rewrite each sentence. Replace the underlined words with a contraction or a possessive.

5. The party is at the house belonging to Brendan.
   The party is at Brendan's house.
6. Please do not come late.
   Please don't come late.

Page 69

Contractions and Possessive Nouns

A contraction is a shortened form of a word or words. An apostrophe replaces the dropped letter or letters in a contraction. Possessive nouns show that a person, place, or thing has or owns something. Add an apostrophe (') and an **s** to make a singular possessive noun.

Contraction	Possessive
Let's go to the store.	**Jason's** friend wants a new belt.

Rewrite each sentence. Replace the underlined words with a contraction.

1. I am looking for red pants. _I'm looking for red pants._
2. She is going to buy jeans. _She's going to buy jeans._
3. Where is the closest store? _Where's the closest store?_

Rewrite each sentence. Replace the underlined words with a possessive.

4. The shoe size of Michelle is smaller than mine.
   Michelle's shoe size is smaller than mine.
5. The manager of the store was helpful.
   The store's manager was helpful.

Page 70

Capitalize Titles and Names, Days, and Months

A proper noun names a specific person, place, or thing. Each main word in a proper noun should begin with a capital letter. The titles and names of people, the days of the week, and the months of the year are proper nouns.

Title and Name	Day	Month
Ms. Olivia Trent	Sunday	January

Circle the proper noun in each sentence. Then write it correctly on the line.

1. Our principal's name is (ms. lana gomez). _Ms. Lana Gomez_
2. Have you met (officer kevin paul)? _Officer Kevin Paul_
3. I have an appointment with my dentist, (dr. don costa).
   Dr. Don Costa

Circle whether each proper noun names a day or a month. Then write it correctly on the line.

4. wednesday _Wednesday_ Day **(Month)** — Day
5. july _July_ Day **(Month)**
6. november _November_ Day **(Month)**

Page 71

Capitalize Geographic Names

Geographic names of specific places are proper nouns. Each main word in a proper noun should begin with a capital letter.

Geographic Names
Brooklyn Bridge
North Carolina
San Francisco

Circle the geographic name in each sentence. Then write it correctly on the line.

1. I am going on a trip to (greenville). _Greenville_
2. It is a city in the state of (south carolina). _South Carolina_
3. I went camping in (yosemite national park).
   Yosemite National Park
4. The park is in (california). _California_
5. There are many musicals to see in (new york city).
   New York City
6. The capital city is (albany). _Albany_
7. Someday, I want to visit (france). _France_

Answer Key

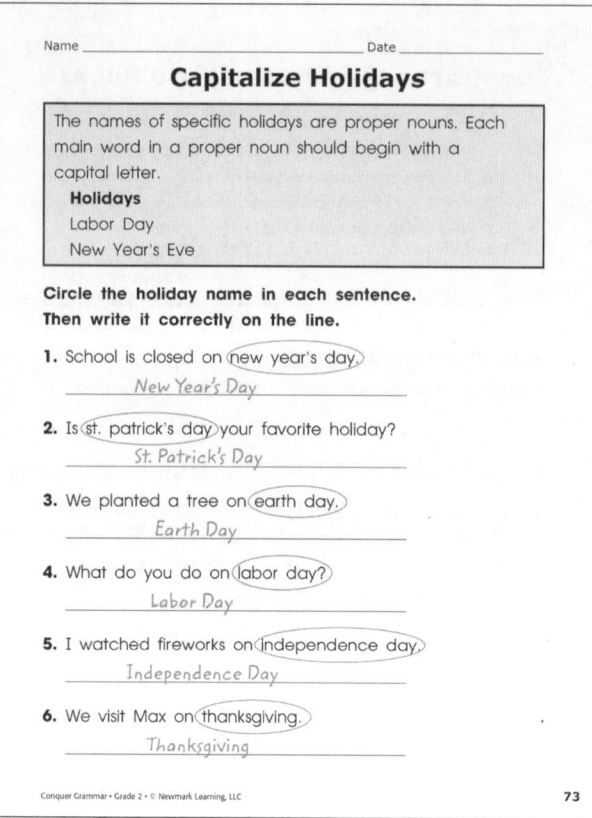

Answer Key

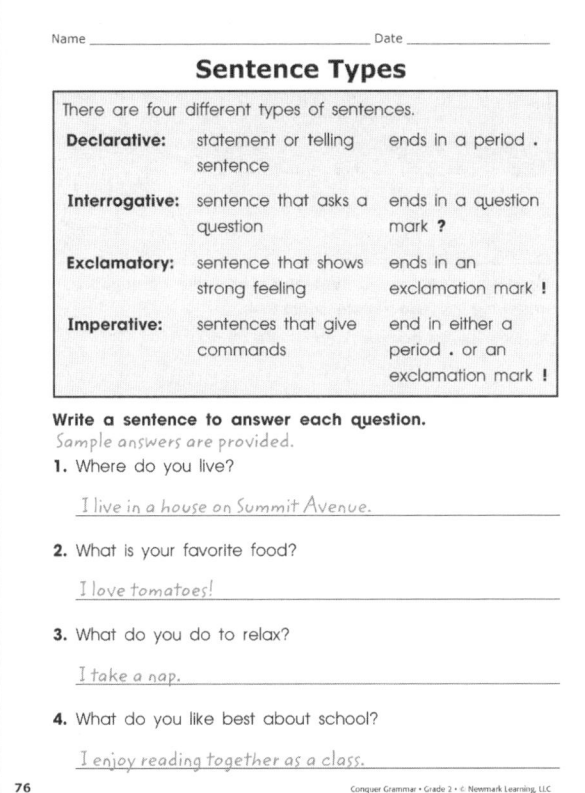

Page 76

Page 77

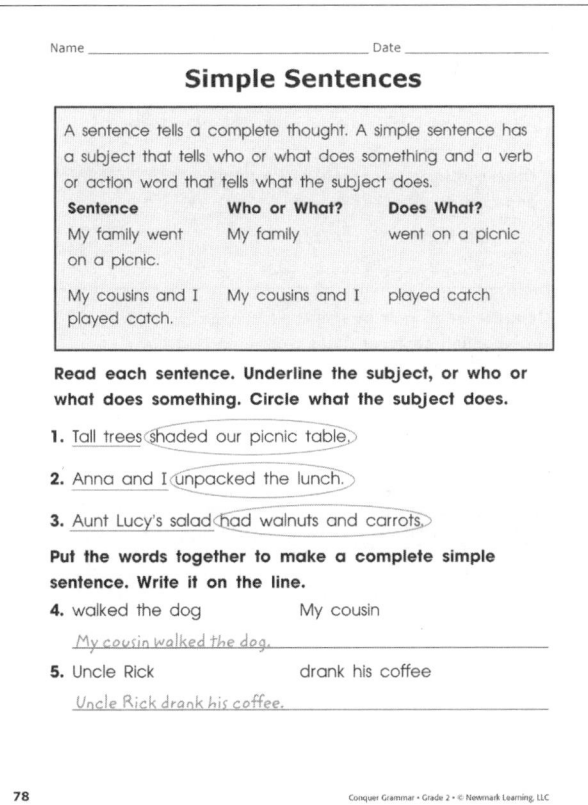

Page 78

Page 79

Answer Key

Page 80

Compound Sentences

A compound sentence is made up of two simple sentences that are joined by a comma and a conjunction, such as **and**, **but**, **or**, or **so**.
I live in the desert. I like to hike.
I live in the desert, **and** I like to hike.

Read each compound sentence. Circle the conjunction. Then write the two simple sentences that make up the compound sentence.

1. The park is crowded,(but) we have fun.
   The park is crowded.   We have fun.
2. We go down the slide,(and) we play on the swings.
   We go down the slide.   We play on the swings.
3. I find flowers,(and) Jess sees a puppy.
   I find flowers.   Jess sees a puppy.
4. It is time to go,(but) we will be back.
   It is time to go.   We will be back.
5. I want to go skiing,(but) I hurt my knee.
   I want to go skiing.   I hurt my knee.

Page 81

Compound Sentences

A compound sentence is made up of two simple sentences that are joined by a comma and a conjunction, such as **and**, **but**, **or**, or **so**.
I like music. I like to read.
I like music, **and** I like to read.

Read each compound sentence. Circle the conjunction. Underline the two simple sentences.

1. Ryan lost his backpack,(and) José found it.
2. Kayla likes nonfiction,(but) Daniel likes folktales.
3. I will meet you at the park,(or) I will see you later.

Combine each pair of simple sentences to make a compound sentence. Add a comma and the conjunction *and* or *but*. Write the compound sentence on the line.

4. Blake called on the phone.   I answered.
   Blake called on the phone, and I answered.
5. We got on our bikes.   We rode to the store.
   We got on our bikes, and we rode to the store.
6. She got some crackers.   I bought cheese.
   She got some crackers, but I bought cheese.

Page 82

Compound Sentences

A compound sentence is made up of two simple sentences that are joined by a comma and a conjunction, such as **and**, **but**, **or**, or **so**.
Mom bought a new vase. It was too small.
Mom bought a new vase, **but** it was too small.

Combine each pair of simple sentences to make a compound sentence. Add a comma and the conjunction *and* or *but*. Write the compound sentence on the line.

1. Laura sings.   We listen.
   Laura sings, and we listen.
2. The movie is short.   It is funny.
   The movie is short, and it is funny.
3. We cheer.   We jump.
   We cheer, and we jump.
4. The day is cold.   The sun is out.
   The day is cold, but the sun is out.
5. We walked to the park.   It was closed.
   We walked to the park, but it was closed.

Page 83

Compound Sentences

A compound sentence is formed when two simple sentences are put together. The simple sentences are combined using a comma and a linking word such as **and** or **but**.
I like apples. Wendy likes pears.
I like apples, **but** Wendy likes pears.

Combine each pair of simple sentences to make a compound sentence. Add a comma and the conjunction *and* or *but*. Write the compound sentence on the line.

1. Mom gets a cart.   Regina pushes.
   Mom gets a cart, and Regina pushes.
2. They buy bread.   They buy cheese.
   They buy bread, and they buy cheese.
3. I am not tired.   Chase is sleepy.
   I am not tired, but Chase is sleepy.
4. The mango is fresh.   The bread is old.
   The mango is fresh, but the bread is old.

Answer Key

Page 84

Compound Sentences

A compound sentence is made up of two simple sentences that are joined by a comma and a conjunction, such as **and**, **but**, **or**, or **so**.
  Bo crossed the finish line. The crowd cheered loudly.
  Bo crossed the finish line, **and** the crowd cheered loudly.

Combine each pair of simple sentences to make a compound sentence. Add a comma and the conjunction *and* or *but*. Write the compound sentence on the line.

1. Emma went to dinner.   She ate a tasty meal.
   Emma went to dinner, and she ate a tasty meal.

2. The weather was hot.   The cool water tasted good.
   The weather was hot, so the cool water tasted good.

3. The movie was long.   It was interesting.
   The movie was long, but it was interesting.

4. Ryan ate a pear.   I ate a juicy orange.
   Ryan ate a pear, and I ate a juicy orange.

5. I could go for a walk.   I could play inside.
   I could go for a walk, or I could play inside.

Page 85

Compound Sentences

A compound sentence is made up of two simple sentences that are joined by a comma and a conjunction, such as **and**, **but**, **or**, or **so**.
  It is cool now. It will be warm later.
  It is cool now, **but** it will be warm later.

Combine each pair of simple sentences to make a compound sentence. Add a comma and a conjunction. Write the compound sentence on the line.

1. It snowed today.   The sky is foggy tonight.
   It snowed today, but the sky is foggy tonight.

2. We picked many apples.   Pears aren't in season.
   We picked many apples, but pears aren't in season.

3. We can stay up late.   We can go to sleep.
   We can stay up late, or we can go to sleep.

4. You can wear a sweater.   You can put on a coat.
   You can wear a sweater, or you can put on a coat.

5. Daisy might stay up.   She might read.
   Daisy might stay up, and she might read.

Page 86

Compound Sentences

A compound sentence is made up of two simple sentences that are joined by a comma and a conjunction, such as **and**, **but**, **or**, or **so**.
  I went to the library. I found a good book.
  I went to the library, **and** I found a good book.

Combine each pair of simple sentences to make a compound sentence. Add a comma and a conjunction. Write the compound sentence on the line.

1. We went to the water park.   We had fun.
   We went to the water park, and we had fun.

2. I went down the slide.   Dad swam.
   I went down the slide, and Dad swam.

3. Mom likes tigers.   I like lions.
   Mom likes tigers, but I like lions.

4. We can see snakes.   We can see zebras.
   We can see snakes, or we can see zebras.

5. I am hungry.   I will make a sandwich.
   I am hungry, so I will make a sandwich.

Page 87

Combine Sentences

Two related short sentences can be combined into one sentence in order to eliminate repetition. Use a conjunction such as **and**, **but**, **or**, or **so** to join the two sentences.
  Henry forgot his homework. Henry forgot his lunch.
  Henry forgot his homework **and** his lunch.

Combine each pair of sentences into one sentence.

1. My sister plays the violin. My brother plays the violin.
   My sister and brother play the violin.

2. The cat was hungry. The cat was thirsty.
   The cat was hungry and thirsty.

3. Jorge wore blue jeans. Jorge wore a red sweater.
   Jorge wore blue jeans and a red sweater.

4. Addison has a new notebook. Addison has a new pencil.
   Addison has a new notebook and a new pencil.

5. Zoe opened the door. Zoe opened the window.
   Zoe opened the door and the window.

Conquer Grammar • Grade 2 • © Newmark Learning, LLC

Answer Key

Page 88

Dictionaries

Use a dictionary to check the spelling, pronunciation, part of speech, and meaning of a word. Words in a dictionary are listed in alphabetical order, from **a** to **z**. When two words begin with the same letter, they are alphabetized by the second letter.

> **ball** (BAUL) *noun* a round object that can be thrown, hit, or kicked
> **blink** (BLINK) *verb* to close and open your eyes fast

Read each group of words. Circle the word that would come first in a dictionary.

1. light — loss — (late)
2. envy — (empty) — ever
3. (flug) — free — foot

Write the words in alphabetical order.

4. trash — tires — tummy — *tires, trash, tummy*
5. poor — plastic — peace — *peace, plastic, poor*
6. share — snack — skip — *share, skip, snack*
7. gym — gem — glow — *gem, glow, gym*

Page 89

Dictionaries

Print dictionaries have two guide words on every page. The first guide word represents the first word on the page. The second guide word represents the last word on the page.

> large • last
> **lark** (LARK) *noun* 1. a small brown bird
> 2. a harmless prank
> **lasso** (LA-soh) *noun* a rope with a large loop at the end

For each set of guide words, circle the word that would be on the dictionary page.

1. hungry • hut — horses — (hurt) — help
2. anger • annoy — (animal) — America — asleep
3. village • viper — vest — (violin) — voice
4. class • coat — curl — crash — (club)
5. kick • knife — (knee) — koala — key
6. divide • dollar — dye — (doctor) — damp
7. man • meal — mouse — mild — (maze)

Page 90

Dictionaries

Use a dictionary to check the spelling, pronunciation, part of speech, and meaning of a word. Words in a dictionary are listed in alphabetical order. When two words begin with the same letter, they are alphabetized to the second letter. Print dictionaries have two guide words on every page. The first guide word is the first word on the page, the second is the last word on the page.

> **pester • pheasant**
> **pester** (PES-ter) *verb* to annoy someone
> **pet** (PET) *noun* a tame animal; *verb* to stroke
> **pheasant** (FEH-zunt) *noun* a large bird with a long tail

Write the words in alphabetical order. Remember to alphabetize to the second letter.

1. rain — road — rest — *rain, rest, road*
2. melon — man — moose — *man, melon, moose*
3. scrape — stink — shade — *scrape, shade, stink*

For each set of guide words, circle the word that would be on the dictionary page.

4. box • branch — blue — (brain) — butterfly
5. line • load — (lizard) — lunch — leave
6. angry • apple — arrow — actor — (apart)

Page 91

Formal and Informal Language

Formal language consists of complete sentences and standard grammar. Use formal language in an essay or a letter to the editor. Informal language consists of incomplete sentences and slang. Use informal language in friendly pieces of writing, such as an e-mail or a letter to a friend.

Formal	Informal
Good night, Miss Lopez.	Bye Ashley. I'm out!
In my opinion, this is correct.	I think it's OK, you know?

Circle whether the language in each example is formal or informal.

1. Good morning, Mr. Mayor. May we ask you about the election?
   (Formal) — Informal
2. Hey! Did you see the cool rainbow? It was awesome!
   Formal — (Informal)
3. Weather experts are expecting clear weather.
   (Formal) — Informal
4. Our plans are totally amazing. I'm super excited!
   Formal — (Informal)